Visual Basic® for Network Applications

Visual Basic® for Network Applications

Simon Collin

Digital Press
Boston • Oxford • Johannesburg • Melbourne • New Delhi • Singapore

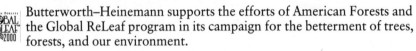
ISBN 1-55558-173-0

The publisher offers special discounts on bulk orders of this book. For information, please contact:

Manager of Special Sales
Butterworth–Heinemann
225 Wildwood Avenue
Woburn, MA 01801-2041
Tel: (781) 904-2500
Fax: (781) 904-2620

For information on all Digital Press publications available, contact our World Wide Web home page at: **http://www.bh.com/digitalpress**

Order number: EY-W931E-DP

10 9 8 7 6 5 4 3 2 1

Design and composition by ReadyText, Bath, UK
Printed in the United States of America

Contents

Introduction

This book covers the programming techniques that you can use to support network resources from within a Visual Basic® (VB) application. Why do you need this book? Well, in its basic form, VB includes few ways of integrating with a networked environment. If you want to find out what else is on the network, link applications, or delve deep into the low-level network calls, then you will need to look to ways outside the standard VB environment.

In this book I have tried to cover all the main techniques that a developer faced with a network challenge will need to understand. If you are writing a simple application to take advantage of Windows® network resources, then these functions are covered; if you want to work with Novell NetWare or NetBIOS networks, these are also covered.

I have also set aside several chapters to cover the various advanced communications methods available on a network—generically termed interprocess communications. For example, if you want to write a groupware product and allow one user to alert all the other users of an appointment, you could use a variety of features: I cover Network DDE, mailslots, named pipes, and basic NetBIOS.

Figure I.1:
Visual Basic makes it very easy to create custom email applications.

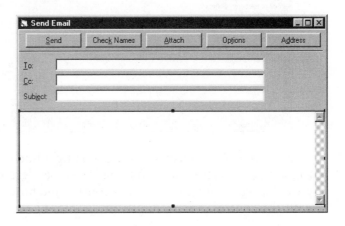

One of the main uses of VB is as a rapid development tool for front-ends. This is particularly relevant with electronic mail applications that might need to "hide" an unfriendly mainframe text-based mail system with a VB application. I have covered email extensively, both from the native MAPI format and from the open SMTP/POP3 standards used over TCP/IP networks (such as an Internet or intranet).

Lastly, once you have tackled the network challenge, there are still multiuser worries ahead for the network developer. I cover the ways in which you can install and distribute an application over the network, using the Windows User Profiles and System Policies to your advantage, and how to manage shared database files and locking.

Writing network applications

To create a network-aware VB program you need to look to API functions. Visual Basic does not have many network functions built into its command set, although it does include the MAPI control for email, the Internet control for TCP/IP, and support for remote object automation in some versions of VB. However, for general-purpose network tasks, such as mapping a drive or printer or listing connections, you can use the API command set that is available within Windows. I describe all of these API calls and show how to use them in Chapter 2.

Figure I.2:
API calls provide one way of accessing network resources.

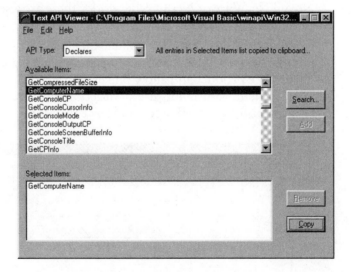

For more advanced techniques, you might find it easier (or essential) to use a third-party control. A number of cases describe the basic principles of programming without the control and how simple life becomes with the control. For example, programming with NetWare is made easier thanks to the free NWCALL.DLL library that Novell supplies developers. However, it is not wrapped in a custom control so you will still need to use API calls to its functions. For techniques such as Net-BIOS and mailslots, you can use the native Windows API functions, but these are complex, so I would recommend using a commercial control component. After all, VB is supposed to be used for rapid development, not long, drawn-out low-level programming.

Which version of VB?

All the techniques I describe work with VB 4 and 5. In the case of the TCP/IP (Internet) programming, I have assumed that developers will use the Microsoft Control Pack, which is available for VB 4 and 5 (and has now been taken over by NetMasters).

Figure I.3:
Microsoft's
popular suite
of Internet
components
is now
supplied by
NetMasters.

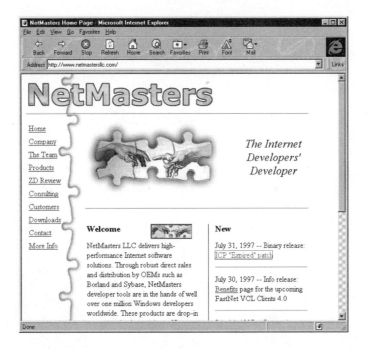

In general, the simple network functions will work with any version of Windows (back to 16-bit Windows for Workgroups), while the more complex APIs will only work with 32-bit Windows. I have pointed out which version of Windows is required to support the call, but I have not included any functions that will only run under NT.

Networking Windows

Introduction

In the rest of the book I describe the methods of accessing network
resources (such as drives and printers) from within Visual Basic. Some
methods use standard VB controls, others resort to the Windows API,
but all are covered. I have also covered the main task that VB is used for
in a network environment: electronic mail. So far, all these features can
be accessed by any user with most versions of VB including 16-bit VB
and VB 5.

However, before launching into the problems of LAN programming, I will use the luxury of this chapter to explain the way in which
you can configure your Windows network resources so that you can
make the most of them inside VB. Once you have created your network
application, you'll need to distribute it over the network; the second
half of this chapter is dedicated to the problems of distributing your
application over a LAN.

Windows 95 as a network platform

Windows 95 supports a number of different network client types
straight from the box; it includes network client software that allows
Windows to use the network resources offered by the networks.
Together with these network clients, Windows also supports a range of
network protocols that define the way data is transferred over the network. By default, there is support for NetBEUI (Microsoft's own), IPX
(Novell), TCP/IP (for Unix and Internet), VINES (for Banyan networks),
PATHWORKS (for DEC systems), and DLC (for IBM computers). The
range of network clients supported are:

- Windows NT
- Windows for Workgroups

- LAN Manager 2.*x* or compatible (includes LAN Server, PATHWORKS) or later
- LANtastic 5.0 or later
- VINES 5.52 or later
- NetWare 3.11 or later
- SunSoft PC-NFS 5.0 or later

Although Windows supports these networks, it generally only provides basic functionality and you will also need client software from the network vendor in order to carry out the other network functions. The beauty of Windows 95 is that your PC can support several different protocols linked to a single network client; for example, to connect to different servers running the same operating system over different protocols.

Windows 95: The network components

To allow Windows 95 to connect to a network, you need to install and configure four basic networking components: the type of network client to use, the type of network adapter that's installed, the network protocol used, and the network services offered by this workstation.

Figure 1.1:
Windows 95 provides good client network configuration.

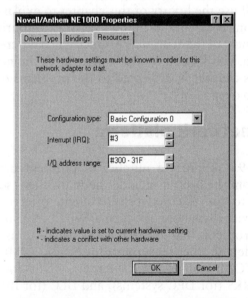

Once installed, either from during Windows installation or from the Control Panel, you can start to configure the components to set their properties and so customize the workstation for the network. These properties will configure the network client, adapter, protocol and services, identify the computer on the network, and provide security and access control. These properties will also be available to your VB application and you can, to a limited extent, change these settings.

TIP

In order to configure the workstation for more than one user, you should use the Windows 95 Profiles feature. This lets several different users have totally different configurations, rights, and network settings stored on one workstation. For more details on Profiles, see later in this chapter.

Configuring network components

To see the current settings and to configure this copy of Windows 95 ready for connection to a network, you'll need to see the settings for the various network components that have been installed (client, adapter, protocol, services).

Figure 1.2:
Setting up
network access
to one or many
types of
network.

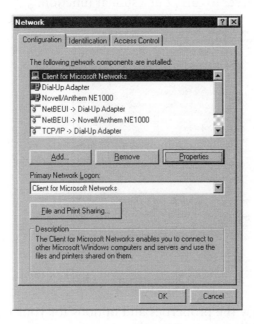

To see the properties for these components, open the Control Panel (*Start ▸ Settings ▸ Control Panel*) and then double-click on the Network icon. As a shortcut to pop up these properties, highlight the Network Neighborhood icon on the Desktop, click the right mouse button, and select the Properties menu option.

There are three main pages within the Network icon—Configuration, Identification, and Access Control. The first, Configuration, shows the network components that have been installed.

Network client

Windows 95 can support as many 32-bit network client components as you care to install, but will only allow one older real-mode network client to be installed at any one time. The reason is that the new 32-bit clients need no real-mode code, whereas the older clients normally only operate in real-mode.

Each network client has a number of options that can be set—these depend on the type of client and the particular network you are connecting to. As an example, I'll use the Microsoft Network Client that would be used for NT or Windows 95 networks, but to see how the other clients can be configured, see Chapter 4 on connecting Windows 95 to different brands of network, such as Novell NetWare. In general, the main difference for the client options is that NetWare users select a preferred server to validate the login, whereas Microsoft users select a domain server to carry out a similar function.

Figure 1.3:
Setting up the way a client shell logs on to a server.

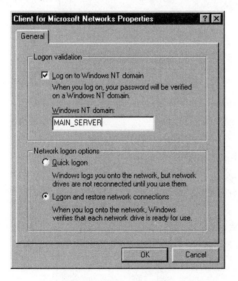

To view the properties and options for your network client, highlight the client name from the network component list of the Network icon and click on the Properties button below the list. This displays the pages associated with this client. In the case of a Microsoft Network client, there's only one General page of options that can be set.

Network adapter

Click on Add and then select a network adapter from the list of components and you'll see the range of adapters that are supported. If your adapter is not supported, you should get a Windows 95 driver from the manufacturer or your dealer (or look on CompuServe).

Network protocol

The Setup program will automatically install the default protocol that's linked to the network client you have chosen. For example, if you choose a Novell NetWare client, it will install Novell's IPX/SPX protocol. Similarly, for Microsoft networks, Windows will install the Net-BEUI protocol.

If you have a standard network to which you are linking the workstation, then there's no need to change the protocol. However, if you are linking to multiple networks, to a host computer, or to a mixed protocol setup, choose the protocol accordingly.

Network service

Network services provide enhanced functions for a particular network. Microsoft supplies a number of services with Windows, or you might have service components from other suppliers or vendors that you want to add.

Figure 1.4:
Several special processes are supplied with Windows 95 that work over a network.

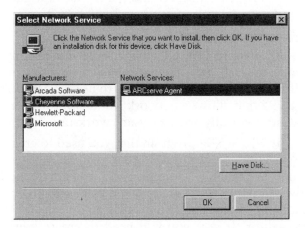

If you select the Add button, then choose Network service, you'll see that there are three basic services available: Arcada Software—a backup agent; Cheyenne Software—another backup agent; and Microsoft—file and printer sharing for either Novell NetWare or Microsoft networks.

In addition to these three basic services, there are further advanced network services aimed at the network administrator. These include

other backup agents, an SNMP agent, and a remote Registry agent—
these are all stored in the ADMIN directory on the CD-ROM version of
Windows 95. To view or install any of these components, click on the
Have Disk button and browse through the CD-ROM contents.

Installing your network applications

Once you have created a new VB application that makes use of your
company's network, you have the rather more difficult job of installing
the application, together with the library files, components, and data
files, onto each of your user's workstations. Sure, VB has the Setup Wizard, but this cannot cope with some of the problems that a network will
throw up.

Local Windows 95

If each user is running a copy of Windows from their local hard drive,
you have it easy! You could add a line to a login script (see below)—if
you have a central server—and use this to copy the new files into place
on each workstation. As a second option, the VB Setup Wizard will
allow you to create a setup utility and produce a disk image of all the
files required for the application. Once you have this disk image, copy it
to the network file server and tell the users where the SETUP utility is
stored.

Shared Windows 95

For installations where there is a server-based copy of Windows that is
shared by each user, then you need a new scheme to distribute your
software. The way around this is to use the MSBATCH feature of Windows 95 that allows a network administrator to create a batch file that
will automatically update a user's workstation configuration.

The NETSETUP program that you used to create the shared server-
based copy of Windows gave you an option to create a basic
MSBATCH.INF file—a simple text file of commands that installed Windows onto the client computers. If you used this option when originally
setting up Windows, then it's time to find the INF file and fire up your
text editor. If not, you will need to create your own INF file from
scratch, which is not too difficult.

The MSBATCH.INF file is read together with any other INF files
when SETUP is run. You can run the SETUP program either from the
command line or from a login script or from a DOS batch file, making it
a very flexible way of updating components on workstations.

In addition to MSBATCH.INF, the Windows SETUP program will look for the following INF files that define how various specific parts of the custom installation work:

MSBATCH.INF	This replaces SETUP.INF and SETUP.SHH from Windows for Workgroups and defines custom system and file settings.
NETDET.INI	This replaces CONTROL.INF and lists incompatible Novell drivers or NetWare TSRs. Setup can automatically handle any other exceptions.
APPS.INF	This defines PIF configuration files for applications launched from Windows.
WRKGRP.INI	Defines membership to workgroups within a network.

Together with these INF and INI files, SETUP will check to see if there is a System Policy that will dictate how the Desktop settings are configured (see page 22 for more on System Policies).

Creating a custom setup script

To install your new application, you need to create your own MSBATCH.INF file; the default copy of this file is stored with the source files on the server, and the custom setup scripts for individual PCs are stored in the users' home directory on the server. There are three ways in which you can create a custom setup script that allow you to produce a "quick and dirty" script or a comprehensive but more laborious script.

The simplest way to create a custom script is to use the Server-based Setup program (described earlier). The principle behind this is that you define the major components and settings that you want to implement from within the Setup program and then save these selections to disk as a script file. Once you have this basic generated script file you can edit it using a standard text editor.

Steps to generate a basic MSBATCH.INF file:

1. Start the server-based Setup utility, and click on the Make Script button.
2. Enter the name MSBATCH.INF and the server location where you want to store this default script.
3. Define the custom properties for this default script using the check boxes in the properties tree displayed.

Custom properties for the default script

The Server-based Setup program allows you to define the custom parameters that will be recorded in the setup script using a series of check boxes (similar to the way in which System Policies are edited). The main properties that can be edited are covered below.

Setup Options Defines the type of installation that will be used and defines the level of user input during the process

- *Automated Install*—defines whether user input is allowed during installation
- *Setup Mode*—selects whether this is a custom or compact installation
- *Create Emergency Disk*—defines whether setup will create a security boot disk
- *Install verification*—if set to verify, will go through the motions, but not copy files

Install Location Defines the location where the files will be copied

- *Install Directory*—sets the InstallDir value to the install destination path
- *Server based setup*—defines whether Windows is installed on the server or locally

Name and Organization

- *Display name page*—if set to zero the name and organization panel is not displayed
- *Name*—specifies the user name
- *Organization*—specifies the organization name

Network Options Defines basic network component options

- *Display network pages*—if set to zero, prevents the network configuration dialog being displayed
- *Clients to install*—defines the list of network clients to install (separate each by a comma). The first client in the list is used as the default client. Use VREDIR for Microsoft networks, NWREDIR for MS client for NetWare or NETX, or VLM for Novell client for NetWare.

Client for Windows Networks

- *Validated Login*—if set, only allows network login if the user is validated by a domain server

- *Logon Domain*—sets the domain name of the server that will validate the user

Client for NetWare Networks

- *Preferred Server*—sets the preferred NetWare server name that will validate the user
- *First Network Drive*—defines the first drive letter that can be used for network resources

Protocols

- *Protocols to Install*—defines a list of protocols to install (separate each by a comma). The first in the list is used as the default protocol. Use NWLINK for IPX/SPX, NETBEUI for Microsoft NetBEUI, or MSTCP for Microsoft TCP/IP.

Net Cards

- *Net cards to Install*—defines a list of network drivers to install (separate each by a comma). Try to avoid using this setting; instead leave it to Windows to automatically detect the driver.

Services

- *Services to Install*—defines a list of network services to install (separate each by a comma). For file and print sharing use either VSERVER for support of MS networks or NWSERVER for support of NetWare networks.

File and Printer Sharing for NetWare Networks

- *SAP Browsing*—if set, enables SAP advertising for this PC
- *Browse Master*—defines whether this PC can be a browse master and so enables workgroup advertising

File and Printer Sharing for Microsoft Networks

- *LMAnnounce*—allows other computers running MS LAN Manager to see this PC
- *Browse Master*—specifies whether this PC can be a browse master. Normally, this is set to Auto, allowing Windows to decide.

Identification

- *Computer Name*—defines the unique name for this PC
- *Workgroup*—defines the workgroup to which this PC belongs

- *Description*—sets the text line that describes this PC

Access Control

- *Security Type*—defines whether this PC implements share or user-level security
- *Pass-through agent*—defines the server that will validate user-level security

System Components

- *Various device types*—defines the section within the INF file that contains the descriptions for other specific devices. Try not to use this command; instead, leave it to Windows to auto-detect these components.

Most Recently Used Paths

- *Most Recently Used Path*—the UNC paths for four paths that can be used during setup

Installing applications from MSBATCH.INF

Now that you have your copy of MSBATCH.INF ready to run, you need to understand how it can be used to install your own applications. This part of the equation is carried out using the INF Installer utility, which allows you to install any application that is supplied with an INF file from within the setup script. The utility works by using a command that will install the application according to its own INF file.

To use the INF Installer's "run once" feature (which runs the application's INF file once), start INF Installer by running INFINST. If you are using INFINST to add system components, you must make sure that you have first installed the system files.

Running a setup script

Now that you have created a setup script, you can run it by using the SETUP command line instruction: SETUP MSBATCH.INF. Make sure that you include the full UNC path to the INF file if it is not in the local Windows source directory.

TIP

To make the whole process invisible to the user, and to save going to each desk, add the SETUP MSBATCH.INF command to the login file to run it automatically.

Defining the client's machine directory

Here's a final piece of information that will be useful if you are using a shared copy of Windows stored on a server. In this installation, each user will have his own unique Machine Directory that is used to hold some configuration information in addition to the local directory and the shared source file directory. The Machine Directory doesn't contain much, but it holds the INI files (including WIN.INI), the client's Registry files, spool printing folder and the INI files that define the Desktop and Start button settings. (If the client is diskless or has only a floppy drive, the Machine Directory also contains the swap file and TEMP folder.)

To define the location of the Machine Directory for a single PC, use the Server-based Setup utility (described above). Click on the Set Up Machine button and select the "one machine" radio button. You can now type in the full UNC path for this PC's Machine Directory.

If you are installing several machines, it is probably easier to create a text file that contains the computer name and the full UNC path to this computer's Machine Directory. The Server-based Setup utility can use this (via the multiple machines option) to automate the process of creating Machine Directories.

Once you have defined the location of the Machine Directory, your VB application can use this to access any INI files it requires—although this should always be done using the API calls that return the official locations of the \WINDOWS directories (see Chapter 2 for more details on accessing system network information).

User Profiles

In much of this book you will see that I mention User Profiles and ways in which a command modifies or reads information from the Profile. A User Profile is, as it sounds, personal settings that are stored in a file; the settings are stored in the USER.DAT file, which is part of the Registry.

Although User Profiles take a little more time for the supervisor to set up and manage, they are well worth the trouble, since they can provide a range of benefits: multiple users can share the same PC—as each one logs on, his own User Profile is retrieved and the Desktop and network settings changed accordingly. A wandering user can log in to any PC on the network and automatically have his own Desktop displayed. You can, as the supervisor, set up company-wide User Profiles that define a simple Desktop that's easy for new users to manage and easy for you to support (this feature is rather like the old INI settings of Windows that allowed a supervisor to limit the actions within Program Manager).

Figure 1.5:
User Profiles
allow multi-
ple users to
each configure
one PC.

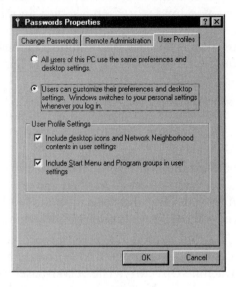

NOTE

If you want to use the User Profiles for roving users, to allow them to log in to any workstation, you must be running 32-bit client software on the workstations and set up a home directory for each user on the network.

User Profiles are a very powerful feature of Windows 95, but it can be overkill to implement this on a user's workstation. The alternative is System Policies, which allow more subtle and selective changes to users and network-wide settings; System Policies are discussed in the next section.

When to use User Profiles

User Profiles take control of a user's environment settings away from the user. As you'll see later, with System Policies you can control a part of the environment, and leave the user to control the rest. With User Profiles you control all settings. You should also note that User Profiles do not give you control over computer-specific settings, rather they only provide control over user-specific settings (System Policies provide control over both computer- and user-specific settings).

User Profiles are most useful when they are used to separate user's customized Desktops on a shared PC or to allow support or supervisor users to roam around the office, but have access to their familiar customized Desktop wherever they log on.

Trying to separate User Profiles from System Policies can sometimes complicate the matter. For example, if you want to use System Policies to configure user-specific settings, then you will need to enable User Profiles. In conclusion, User Profiles allow you to control user-specific settings; they are also used by the more wide-ranging System Policies features to control user-specific settings.

User Profiles can be set at any time using the Control Panel tools, but they can also be set up using scripts during the initial Windows setup process. When you install Windows 95, you can define a series of install scripts that automatically changes workstation settings according to the user details.

How User Profiles work

User Profiles store user-specific settings including preferences, options and configuration details for a particular user. These settings are stored in the USER.DAT file, which forms one half of the Registry (along with SYSTEM.DAT). If you have started to look at the Registry, the User Profile includes all the information within the Hkey_Current_User section. If you have not got to grips with the Registry, this means the information that's provided by any of the Control Panel settings for the Desktop (its color, pattern, font, shortcuts, etc).

As well as the shortcuts placed directly on the Desktop, a User Profile also includes the settings recorded when an application is installed and writes settings directly to the Registry. Lastly, the User Profile also includes network connection settings, particularly persistent connections, together with the details of the most recently used resources.

Figure 1.6:
Logging on to
a network.

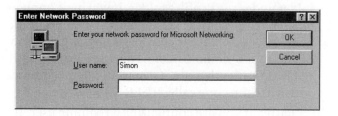

When a user logs in to a computer, Windows 95 looks through the Registry to see if the user has a local User Profile; if it doesn't find one, it will then look for a profile in the user's home directory on the network server. If Windows cannot find a profile either locally or on the server, it will create a new User Profile on the local drive using the default settings. If Windows does find a profile, it will use the most recent version of either the local or server-based User Profile.

When the user logs off the computer, any changes he made are recorded in the profile and the local or network-based User Profiles are updated. Note that if a user logs in on two different workstations he can still use a network-based User Profile, but only the latest changes are recorded. If a user does not log on to the computer, the default User Profile settings are used by Windows.

In order to use User Profiles, the feature has to be enabled on the workstation; once you have done this, a series of folders are created to store each user's preferences. The main folder is called Profiles (a subfolder of Windows) and contains folders for each registered user of the workstation. Each user's folder has four sub-folders stored within it: Desktop, Recent, Start Menu and Programs. As you might imagine, these four folders hold the settings for the various parts of the Windows settings.

Contents of the user's home directory:

- USER.DAT contains the user settings for the Registry.
- USER.DA0 is a backup of USER.DAT.
- Desktop folder contains the contents of the Desktop including shortcuts and settings.
- Recent folder contains the recently used resources; the same as the *Start ▸ Documents* menu item.
- Start Menu folder contains the items that are included in the Start Menu button.
- Programs sub-folder contains program-specific settings recorded to the Registry when the applications are installed.

When a new user logs into the computer, it creates a new user home folder under the Profiles folder. If you have implemented a standard set of User Profiles, these are then implemented. If the user can customize his own Desktop, these custom settings are saved in the four sub-folders of the user's home folder. The User Profile settings are stored in a USER.DAT file; this file is stored in the user's home directory together with a backup copy called USER.DA0.

Lastly, if you are configuring a roaming user, his or her home directory and User Profile folder structure is stored on a network server and the details downloaded to the local workstation whenever he or she logs in. (Note that although Windows 95 and Windows NT offer similar functions, a roaming user can only log in on a Windows 95 workstation and download his or her User Profile.)

Installing User Profiles

In order to use User Profiles on a computer, the feature has to be enabled. You can either do this during the main Windows installation procedure, or later from the Control Panel. To enable the User Profiles on a computer, select the Passwords icon in the Control Panel and select the User Profile page tag. There are two radio-button options; choose the second, which allows users to customize their preferences and desktop settings (i.e., using User Profiles). Two check boxes below the main options give you a choice on what to include within the User Profile such as the desktop icons (for shortcuts) and the contents of the Start menu. In order to activate User Profiles, you need to restart the computer. Note that if you want to disable User Profiles for a computer, select the Passwords icon in the Control Panel, select the User Profiles page tag and select the first radio button.

Figure 1.7:
Selecting the
first User
Profile setting
ensures that
network
options can be
configured for
each user.

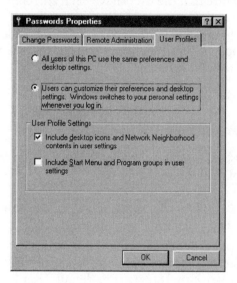

TIP

If you want to change all the workstations to enable the User Profiles feature, you should use a System Policy—see later on how to do this.

User Profiles on an NT network

If the local computer is connected to a network based around a server running Windows NT, you can follow the installation process described above. There are just a couple of extra points that you should bear in mind. First, you should use the Client for Microsoft Networks as the primary network logon client within the Network option of Control Panel (this is a native, 32-bit client that allows User Profiles to be downloaded). Second, the User Profiles will be stored on the server, so you should make sure that the users are registered on the server and have the correct rights. The User Profiles folders are stored in the following location: \\logon_server_name\user_home_folder. Note that the PROFILES directory in NT is only used for the NT profiles, not for the Windows 95 profiles.

User Profiles on a NetWare network

If the local computer is connected to a network based around a server running Novell NetWare, you can follow the installation process described above. There are just a couple of extra points that you should bear in mind. First, you should use the Client for NetWare Networks as the primary network logon client within the Network option of Control Panel. Second, the User Profiles will be stored on the server, so you should make sure that the users have been correctly created under NetWare and that they have a MAIL sub-directory (which is created by SYSCON when the user is created). The User Profiles folders are stored in the existing MAIL sub-directory on the SYS volume of the preferred server in the following location:

```
\\preferred_server_name\sys\mail\user_name
```

Setting up a preset default User Profile

One of the useful functions of User Profiles is that they allow a supervisor to control the look of the Desktop for each user. This is particularly useful if you are setting up Windows for new users or if you want to minimize the effort in training. Each workstation will look exactly the same and no customization is permitted.

To carry out this feature, you will need to be connected to a NetWare or NT central server. First, enable User Profiles on each computer (as shown above). Now, create your default User Profile on one computer. You can install the shortcuts you want, remove items, change colors, set up the Start button and so on. All these changes will be recorded to the USER.DAT file.

To turn this one User Profile into a fixed, company-wide profile, simply copy the USER.DAT file and rename it USER.MAN. Copy USER.MAN into each user's home directory (either on the NT or NetWare server). When the users log in, Windows will use the USER.MAN file (MAN stands for Mandatory User Profile).

Using User Profiles on peer networks

Almost all the configuration settings I have described are related to workstations connected to a network based around a central dedicated server running either Microsoft Windows NT server or Novell Net-Ware. It is possible to use User Profiles on a peer-to-peer network based solely on computers running Windows 95, but there are a few problems that you will need to address.

If you want to set up your peer-to-peer network to allow roaming users to log in from any workstation, you have more of a problem than if you are using a central server. The problem is that there is no main home user directory from which Windows can download the user's profile. To get around this, you will need to store the profile folders on a shared computer and then tell the Registry that it should look at this shared folder to download the User Profile files.

First, create a text file on the computer that will store the shared folder that holds the User Profiles of the roaming users. Call the text file ROAMING.INI. It should contain pointers to the home folders for any roaming user. For example, if the folders are all stored on a server called MAIN in a folder called ROAMUSER you would enter the following lines:

```
[Profiles]
Simon = \\MAIN\ROAMUSER\SIMON
John = \\MAIN\ROAMUSER\JOHN
```

This sets up two roaming users, called Simon and John, whose User Profile data will be stored in the \\Main server in the RoamUser folder. Now you need to create these folders and point the Registry at this INI file so that it can be redirected to the correct location (it sounds long-winded, but is straightforward).

Start the Registry Editor and select the Hkey_Local_Machine\Network\Logon sub-key. Select the *Edit ▸ New* menu item and click on the String Value item. Type ShareProfileList as a new string value and press Enter. In the Edit String dialog box, type the full UNC path to the ROAMING.INI file you've created and click on OK.

Now, whenever either Simon or John logs in on this local computer, it will check with the Registry, which will tell it to look on the Main server, which will point it to the User Profiles, which it can then download.

System Policies

System Policies are far more powerful than User Profiles, in that they allow the network supervisor to control access to various programs, applets and commands within Windows 95—so preventing users from doing things that might wreck the computer's setup. In addition, System Policies can also be used to define user settings by changing the User Policies (to do this, the User Policies feature needs to be enabled).

For example, you can use System Policies to prevent a user running a particular application such as starting an MS-DOS session, restricting access to the Control Panel or customizing the Desktop. Because System Policies are a fairly complex and major subject, Microsoft has included a set of template System Policies that you can use, or you can always define your own.

Figure 1.8:
Limiting
access to the
Control Panel
using the
System Policy
Editor.

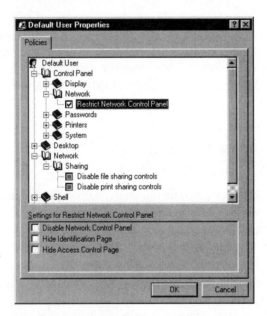

How System Policies work

You start by creating a System Policy file using the System Policy Editor. This policy file is called CONFIG.POL. When a user logs on to a computer, the CONFIG.POL file is executed and this makes any changes to both the USER.DAT and SYSTEM.DAT files that make up the Registry (note that User Profiles only change the USER.DAT file).

When a user logs on to the computer, Windows checks to find the location of the policy file, CONFIG.POL. It then downloads the policies from the server and makes changes to the USER.DAT and SYSTEM.DAT files.

If you have enabled User Profiles on a computer, the update process is slightly different: Windows checks to see if there is a User Profile file that matches the user's name. If it finds one, it runs this to modify the user settings. If it does not find a User Profile file, it will apply the default settings.

There is one other twist: using Group Policies. These are System Policies that apply to a network group of users. (See later on how to set up Group Policies.) If Group Policies are enabled, Windows will check to see if the user who has logged on is a member of any groups. If he is, Windows will then download the Group Policy files and apply these to the User Profile.

Figure 1.9: The System Policy Editor allows you to configure lower level network client features.

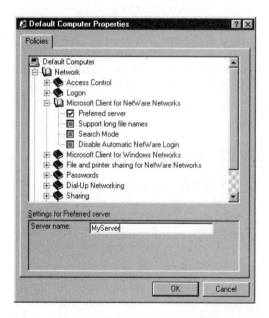

The next step, once the user settings have been configured according to the various policy and profile files, is to set up the computer according to the System Policy. Windows now checks to see if there is a Computer Policy for this particular computer name. If it finds a policy file for the computer, it downloads the policy and configures the Desktop and application settings accordingly in the SYSTEM.DAT part of the Registry. If no Computer Policy is found, it uses the default settings.

Windows defaults to downloading the System Policies automatically when a user logs in. The System Policies will only be downloaded

from the primary NT logon server or the preferred NetWare server—
no other servers will be searched.

Installing System Policy Editor

Before you use System Policies, you need to install the Editor—
although it might seem tempting to make changes to the Registry using
a text editor, do not! It's not like the old INI files, and Windows will
become corrupted if you do not use the Editor. To install the System
Policy Editor, insert the distribution CD-ROM and start the Add/
Remove Programs icon in the Control Panel. Click on the Windows
Setup page tag and click on the Have Disk button. Select Browse and
point to the \ADMIN\APPTOOLS\POLEDIT folder on the CD-ROM.
Click OK and the System Policy Editor will be added to the options that
can be installed. Select it and click on Install.

Using System Policy Editor

Once you have installed the System Policy Editor, you'll notice that no
entry is made in the Start button menu, so to run the System Policy Editor click on *Start ▸ Run* and enter POLEDIT at the command line. You
can then create a shortcut to the program for convenience.

Figure 1.10:
Policies for a
single user,
group and
the basic
computer.

You can use the Editor in two ways: either to directly edit the Registry or to create a policy that can then be run to make changes to the Registry. (Note that you can edit either the local Registry or a Registry on a
remote computer.) If you directly edit the Registry, any changes will be
reflected immediately. If you create a policy, this will only take effect
when the specified user logs in and the policy is downloaded.

Three States of Registry Options
When you are editing the Registry or editing a System Policy, you must
be aware that each Registry option has three possible states: on, off and
grayed. Although the options look like a normal check box, you actually cycle through these three states as you click on the check box. It's

very important to make sure that you are using the right state for the check box, or you could easily wipe out the user's Registry settings.

- *Checked*—this state, with a tick in the box, means the policy for the option will be used and the user's Registry changed accordingly.
- *Unchecked*—this state, an empty box, means the policy is not implemented and any existing setting is cleared from the user's Registry.
- *Grayed*—this state, a gray box, means that no changes are made to the Registry.

Editing the Registry

This mode of operation of the System Policy Editor is not really to be encouraged! You should use the Control Panel and its relevant applets to make any changes to either the user or system parts of the Registry. If you do really want to edit the Registry, start the Editor and you'll see two icons, one for the USER.DAT user section and one for the SYSTEM.DAT computer section. Double-click on the icon you want to edit and you will have full access to this section. See later in this chapter on how to edit.

Editing a System Policy

Start the Editor and select the *File ▸ New* menu item. The window title bar shows the name of the policy that you've created, and in the main window you'll see two icons representing the two parts that make up the Registry: the user icon represents the USER.DAT file and its options, the computer icon represents the SYSTEM.DAT file and its options.

Double-click one of the icons to view the settings for this part of the Registry. The settings are displayed in a collapsed tree structure and are relatively straightforward to navigate: there are sections for each of the main settings of the user or computer's configuration. Expand this branch to see individual options and you will also see a check box that describes if the policy for this option will be implemented or not (see the box for important details on the check boxes).

Creating a new User Policy

To create a new policy for a user, start the Policy Editor and select the *Edit ▸ Add User* menu item. Type in the name of the user that you want to add and a new user icon appears in the main Editor window. It's the

same process to add a new Computer icon and policy: choose the
Edit ▸ Add Computer menu item.

You can now edit the individual sections of the policy by double-
clicking on the icon and scanning through the tree structure.

There are so many different Policy settings that I cannot cover them
all in this book. However, the descriptions you'll see in the section tree
structures are very clear and backed up by on-line help. As an example,
here is a way of defining how to set the preferred NetWare logon server
for a computer using a System Policy:

Create a new Computer policy using the *Edit ▸ Add Computer* menu
item. Double-click on the Computer icon and move down through the
tree structure to the Network options. Open this view by clicking on
the word Network and move to the tree branch labeled Microsoft Client for NetWare Networks. Double-click on this line and it will expand
to show the various options. If you check the first option, Preferred
Server, you can specify the name of the NetWare server that the computer will use for its primary log in.

Figure 1.11:
*The Microsoft
Client allows
fine-tuning of
its features
using the
System Policy
Editor.*

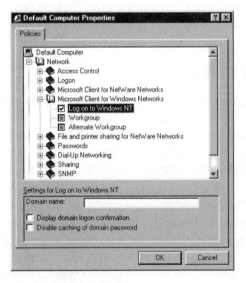

Group System Policies

Group System Policies allow you to define a set of policies that apply to
an existing network group of users (the group must have been created
using system tools, such as SYSCON for a NetWare network).

In order to support Group System Policies, each computer needs to
have a special DLL file installed onto its local drive. This file, called

GROUPPOL.DLL, has to be installed into the Windows folder of each target computer (it is installed when you install System Policy Editor).

To create a new Group policy, start the Editor and choose the *Edit ▸ Add Group* menu item. If you are running user-level security, you'll see a list of available groups, which you can browse to make your choice. Alternatively, if you are using share-level security you need to type in a group name. Double-click on the new policy icon and configure the policy tree as required.

Conclusion

In this chapter, I have covered the ways in which Windows implements the networking functions that you want to access. I have also included information that shows you how to install and manage a networked application using some of the features available under Windows 95— including the powerful System Policies and User Profiles.

Many of the functions that are covered in later chapters will make changes to the Windows 95 Registry, including adding persistent connections and mappings. This chapter will have provided a technical background to the ways in which Windows manages networks, resources, and networked applications.

2

Network Programming

Introduction

There are two distinct ways to integrate your VB application with the network resources available under Windows, and these two methods depend on the version of Windows you are using. If your finished application will run under a 16-bit version of Windows, then you have a hard job ahead. If you are using or delivering to a 32-bit platform (either Windows 95 or NT) your job is made considerably easier thanks to the Win32 API, which provides a usable interface between any application and the network resources.

The big difference is due to the way in which the Windows kernel manages network links. In the 32-bit version, which is a complete operating system, your copy of Windows can support multiple protocols and link to multiple servers and different operating systems. The hard work involved in managing the different data formats is entirely carried out by Windows.

If you are using a 16-bit version of Windows, there are a few basic network functions available via the API, but most of the network calls will have to be carried out in a conversation with the network operating system driver—supplied by the network operating system vendor. For example, if you are linked to a Novell NetWare server, you will need to call functions in the NetWare client DLL supplied by Novell.

In this chapter, I will assume that the majority of developers will be aiming at the 32-bit version of Windows and so I will describe the Win32 API functions in detail. However, I have included comprehensive details of the functions required for 16-bit versions of Windows, especially the NetWare DLL support.

To make it easier to handle these various 16-bit DLL calls, there are several third-party VBX library components that give your application access to network resources; I have covered these later in this chapter.

Windows network API functions

The 16-bit versions of Windows (that is, Windows 3.1 and 3.11—Windows for Workgroups) support three basic API functions that allow the developer to get the name of a network resource, connect to the network resource and break the link to a network resource. The Win32 API library of Windows 95 and NT builds on this and adds another ten functions that allow you to manage the network resources in a more orderly and efficient way; it also provides error detection and includes two standard network dialog boxes.

Figure 2.1:
Visual Basic is supplied with a complete API definition file.

All these API functions will work over any network that is supported by and installed onto Windows. The job of installing the network is carried out from the Install application and the process of configuring the network links is via the Network icon in the Control Panel. Once you have your network client software up and running, you can call the API functions to give your VB application access to the resources. Although it is usual to map network drives using the Explorer utility, you can map them via API calls from your VB application and the same is true when connecting to network printers.

The following are API functions common to Windows 3.1*x* and Windows 95.

- **WNetAddConnection()** Allows the application to connect a local resource to a network resource, for example to connect a drive letter to a shared drive or folder or to connect a printer port to a shared network printer. Any connections created using this function are persistent and Windows will attempt to reconnect to the resource when the user next logs on to the network.
- **WNetCancelConnection()** Cancels a connection to a network resource (applies to connections created with the AddConnection function or connections created by another utility)
- **WNetGetConnection()** Returns the name of the network resources that have been associated with a particular local resource; for example, if you use the argument "F:" the function will return the full shared network path mapped to this drive letter

API functions for Windows 95

The following set of functions are available for the 32-bit versions of Windows and provide far greater flexibility than the earlier three functions. Unless you have to support a 16-bit Windows platform, you should use the following API calls.

- **WNetAddConnection2()** New function that supersedes the previous function (above); it is used to create either persistent or non-persistent mappings between a local resource and a network resource. The main difference between this and the older function is that this now uses the NETRESOURCE custom data type structure that contains all the connection information.
- **WNetCancelConnection2()** New function that supersedes the previous function (above); it is used to cancel a persistent or non-persistent connection and has the advantage that it can be used to cancel a persistent connection that is not currently connected
- **WNetCloseEnum()** Closes the report function (WNetOpenEnum) for a particular network resource
- **WNetConnectionDialog()** Displays a standard dialog box that allows a user to browse and connect network resources
- **WNetDisconnectDialog()** Displays a standard dialog box that allows a user to browse and disconnect network resources
- **WNetEnumResource()** Continues the WNetOpenEnum function and reports back on the available network resources

- **WNetGetLastError()** Returns the last reported extended error code that was triggered by a network function
- **WNetGetUniversalName()** Used to convert a drive and path string into a full network connection string with the server and shared resource name (normally called the universal naming convention—UNC— name)
- **WNetGetUser()** Returns the name of the current logged in user
- **WNetOpenEnum()** Starts a list of a particular type of network resources

Figure 2.2:
The API Viewer makes it easy to find and use APIs.

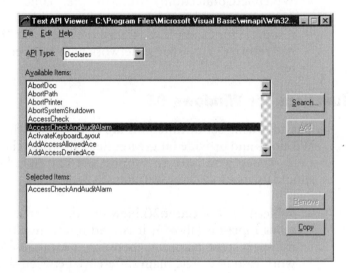

Using Windows API functions

The list of API functions above shows that there is a good range of commands available to any VB developer and, by using the utilities supplied with VB 4 and 5, they are not difficult to use. In order to use any of the API function calls, you need to copy the function name exactly as written and use the correct type and number of arguments. Probably the simplest way of doing this is to copy and paste the function name (with its list of arguments)—Microsoft has kindly included an API function list utility that will do just this.

To use the Text API Viewer utility, open your VB window or folder and look for this application; you will probably see two versions, one for 16-bit Windows and the other for 32-bit Windows. Start the 32-bit version and select the *File ▸ Open* menu option; choose to open the Win32API.txt file that contains all the API command set for the 32-bit Windows API.

Perhaps the best way to use the Text API Viewer is to locate the network functions that you will want to use in your project from the complete API listing; click on the Add button to copy the function into the lower window; finally, click the Copy button to copy your list of network functions to the Clipboard. Now you can turn back to your VB project and paste the function listings into your program.

Any API function calls that you do use will be routed by VB to the MPR.LIB library file that manages the translations between any multiple network types or protocols.

Working with standard VB components

The range of Windows API functions that have been introduced in this chapter are designed to allow an application to control the way local resources connect to shared resources. However, the standard VB components will reflect any existing network connections without any extra code. For example, if you are connected to a network and use the standard Drive listbox component from the VB palette, it will list all the local and mapped network drive letters. Similarly, if you use the standard Print dialog box, it will display the range of local and shared network printer mappings that have been defined elsewhere in Windows.

Figure 2.3:
*A simple form
with drive and
folder list
boxes.*

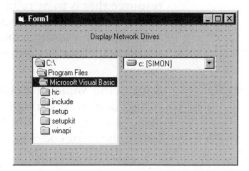

Where the API functions become useful is that it allows the developer to create and break off connections and mappings with shared resources; once the mapping has been created with an API function, you can return to the comfort of the VB components to make use of the new mapping.

The network API functions in detail

WNetAddConnection(...)

`lngReturnValue = `**`WNetAddConnection`**`(strResourceName, strPassword, strLocalName)`

use with	16-bit or 32-bit Windows
used for	allows the application to connect a local resource to a network resource, for example to connect a drive letter to a shared drive or folder or to connect a printer port to a shared network printer. Any connections created using this function are persistent and Windows will attempt to reconnect to the resource when the user next logs on to the network.

parameters	*parameter*	*explanation*
	`strResourceName`	string variable that contains the full network path to the network resource
	`strPassword`	string variable that contains any password required to connect to the network
	`strLocalName`	string variable that contains the local resource that is to be redirected to the network resource; for example "G:" or "LPT1"; if this string is null, a connection is still made but no redirection is carried out
	`lngReturnValue`	returns the value of `ERROR_SUCCESS` if the connection was correctly established; if there was an error, the function returns one of the error codes in Table 2.1.

WNetCancelConnection(...)

`LngReturnVal = `**`WNetCancelConnection`**`(strResourceName, bForce)`

use with	16-bit or 32-bit Windows
used for	cancels a connection to a network resource (applies to connections created with the AddConnection function or connections created by another utility)

parameters	*parameter*	*explanation*
	strResourceName	string variable that contains the name of the local resource being redirected or the name of the network resource that is connected
	bForce	boolean value that, if FALSE, will not complete the action if there are files or jobs open on the connection but, if TRUE, will force disconnection
	lngReturnVal	returns ERROR_SUCCESS if the function completes correctly or one of the error codes shown in Table 2.1.

WNetGetConnection(...)

lngReturnVal = **WNetGetConnection**(strLocalName, strRemoteResource, lngBuffer)

This function will return one of the standard error codes (used by the previous two functions) if there is a network or device error. If the function succeeds, the ERROR_SUCCESS code is returned. If the str-RemoteResource is not big enough (according to the lngBuffer size) to hold the information returned, the information is truncated and the error ERROR_MORE_DATA code is returned.

use with	16-bit or 32-bit Windows
used for	returns the name of the network resources that have been associated with a particular local resource; for example, if you use the argument "F:" the function will return the full shared network path mapped to this drive letter

parameters	*parameter*	*explanation*
	strLocalName	string variable that contains the name of the local device for which we want the network connection path
	strRemoteResource	string variable that the function will use to store the full network path for the resource
	lngBuffer	long variable that defines the size of the strRemoteResource variable (in characters)

WNetAddConnection2(...)

```
LngReturnVal = WNetAddConnection2(nrNetResouce, strPassword, strUserName,
                        lngConnect)
```

use with	32-bit Windows
used for	new function that supersedes the previous function (above); it is used to create either persistent or non-persistent mappings between a local resource and a network resource. The main difference between this and the older function is that this now uses the NETRE-SOURCE custom data type structure that contains all the connection information

parameters	*parameter*	*explanation*
	nrNetResource	the VB custom data type (NETRESOURCE structure) that needs to be defined in your VB code and contains the information described later
	strPassword	string variable that contains any password required to connect to the network; if this is null, the password associated with the user name (below) is used; if it is an empty string, no password is used
	strUserName	string variable that contains the user name to be used in making the connection; if this is null, the resource's default user name is used
	lngConnect	defines the type of connection; if this is set to CONNECT_UPDATE_PROFILE the connection is added to the user profile as a persistent connection; if this is set to zero, the profile is not updated and the connection is not persistent

Using the NETRESOURCE structure

The custom data type that is used in the WNetCancelConnection2() function requires some of the data entries to be filled in before the function will work correctly. Specifically, you need to complete the lngType, strLocalName, strRemoteName and strProvider parts of the structure.

```
Type NETRESOURCE

    lngScope as Long          'scope of structure
    lngType as Long           'type of the resource to be used
    lngDisplayType as Long    'how resources will be displayed
    lngUsage as Long          'resource usage
    strLocalName as String    'name of the local device to be used
    strRemoteName as String   'name of the network resource to
                              'be connected
    strComment as String      'comment field for the provider
    strProvider as String     'name of the provider who
                              'owns the resource
End Type
```

parameter	explanation
structure parameters	
lngType	defines the type of the network resource that we are trying to connect to; if the strLocalName variable contains a local resource name, then this variable can be defined as a drive or printer using the constants:
	RESOURCETYPE_DISK
	and
	RESOURCETYPE_PRINT
	if there is no strLocalName string (in which case, the connection is made but not redirected) then a third option is the constant RESOURCETYPE_ANY
strLocalName	string variable that contains the local resource that is to be redirected to the network resource; for example "G:" or "LPT1"; if this string is null, a connection is still made but no redirection is carried out
strRemoteName	string variable that contains the name of the network resource that is connected
strProvider	defines the name of the provider to connect to; if you are sure of the provider, you can complete this string; otherwise, set it to a null string and Windows will find out and complete the string for you

This function returns `ERROR_SUCCESS` on completion, or one of the standard error codes.

WNetCancelConnection2(...)

`lngReturnVal =` **`WNetCancelConnection2`**`(strLocalName, intUpdate, bForce)`

used with	32-bit Windows
used for	new function that supersedes the previous cancel function (above); it is used to cancel a persistent or non-persistent connection and has the advantage that it can be used to cancel a persistent connection that is not currently connected

parameters	*parameter*	*explanation*
	`strLocalName`	local resource name, such as the drive letter
	`intUpdate`	variable that indicates if the user profile should be updated with information about the cancelled connection; if it is set to zero, the profile is not updated, if set to `CONNECT_UPDATE_PROFILE` the profile is updated. For example, if you want to break a connection but still want it to remain as a persistent connection next time the user logs on, set this to zero
	`bForce`	boolean value that, if `FALSE`, will not complete the action if there are files or jobs open on the connection but, if `TRUE`, will force disconnection

WNetCloseEnum()

Closes the report function (WNetOpenEnum) for a particular network resource

WNetConnectionDialog(...)

`lngReturnVal =` **`WNetConnectionDialog`**`(hWnHandle, lngResourceType)`

used with	32-bit Windows

| used for | displays a standard dialog box that allows a user to browse and connect network resources |

parameters	*parameter*	*explanation*
	hWnHandle	handle to the window that is creating this dialog box; use the form's hWnd property to set this variable
	lngResourceType	type of resource that should be displayed in the dialog box; this can be either drives or printers by setting this variable to either: RESOURCETYPE_DISK *or* RESOURCETYPE_PRINT

The dialog box function will return ERROR_SUCCESS if the connection is successfully made or will return 0xFFFFFFFF if the user presses the cancel button. If the resource requires a password, Windows displays a password entry dialog and attempts to connect again. Other network and resource errors are reported using the standard error codes (see later).

WNetDisconnectDialog(...)

LngReturnVal = **WNetDisconnectDialog**(hWnHandle, lngResourceType)

| used with | 32-bit Windows |

| used for | displays a standard dialog box that allows a user to browse and disconnect network resources |

parameters	*parameter*	*explanation*
	hWnHandle	handle to the window that is creating this dialog box; use the form's hWnd property to set this variable
	lngResourceType	type of resource that should be displayed in the dialog box; this can be either drives or printers by setting this variable to either RESOURCETYPE_DISK *or* RESOURCETYPE_PRINT

The dialog box function will return ERROR_SUCCESS if the connection is successfully made or will return 0xFFFFFFFF if the user presses the cancel button; other network and resource errors are reported using the standard error codes (see later).

WNetEnumResource()

Continues the WNetOpenEnum function and reports back on the available network resources

WNetGetLastError(...)

```
lngReturnVal = WNetGetLastError(lngCode, strDescription, lngDescription,
                                strName, lngName)
```

used with	32-bit Windows
used for	returns the last reported extended error code that was triggered by a network function or the network operating system, so provides network-specific error codes

parameters	*parameter*	*explanation*
	lngCode	error code generated by the network operating system
	strDescription	string describing the error code; if the string variable is too small, the description is truncated
	lngDescription	sets the size of the variable used to store strDescription—make sure that this variable is at least 256-characters long
	strName	name of the network provider (make of the network operating system) that generated the error—for example, Novell
	lngName	sets the size of the variable used to store strName

This function should be used to find out the cause of an error when any of these API network functions returns the value:

ERROR_EXTENDED_ERROR

WNetGetUniversalName()

Used to convert a drive and path string into a full network connection string with the server and shared resource name (normally called the universal naming convention—UNC—name).

WNetGetUser(...)

`lngReturnVal = `**`WNetGetUser`**`(strResourceName, strUserName, lngUserName)`

used with	32-bit Windows
used for	returns the name of the current logged in user
parameters	*parameter* *explanation*

parameter	*explanation*
strResourceName	name of the resource that you want to query to find out its user, for example a drive letter
strUserName	string that is used to store the user name of the resource
lngUserName	long value of the size of the strUserName variable

WNetOpenEnum(...)

`lngReturnVal = `**`WNetOpenEnum`**`(lngScope, lngType, lngUsage, NETRESOURCE)`

used with	Windows 95 and NT
used for	retrieves a list of the structure and components on a section of the network; for example, it can be used to list the server name, disk volume name, shared printers and disks on the server

LngScope   Specifies how deep to look for resources:
- RESOURCE_CONNECTED (all currently connected resources)
- RESOURCE_GLOBALNET (all resources on the network)
- RESOURCE_REMEMBERED (all persistent connections)

FdwType   Specifies the type of resource to enumerate:
- RESOURCETYPE_ANY (all resources)
- RESOURCETYPE_DISK (all disk resources)
- RESOURCETYPE_PRINT (all print resources)

Standard error codes returned by functions

Table 2.1 *Standard error codes*

Constant	Code	Meaning
5&	ERROR_ACCESS_DENIED	access to network resource denied
85	ERROR_ALREADY_ASSIGNED	network resource is already connected
	ERROR_BAD_DEV_TYPE	local device and network device do not match
	ERROR_BAD_DEVICE	incorrect resource name in strLocalName
67	ERROR_BAD_NET_NAME	incorrect resource name in strResourceName
1206	ERROR_BAD_PROFILE	User Profile is incorrect for this connection
	ERROR_BUSY	provider busy so a new connection cannot be made
	ERROR_CANCELLED	attempt to create a connection was cancelled, either by the user, the provider, or for another reason
	ERROR_CANNOT_OPEN_PROFILE	Windows cannot open the User Profile for a persistent connection
	ERROR_DEVICE_ALREADY_REMEMBERED	the User Profile already has an entry for this strLocalName device
1208	ERROR_EXTENDED_ERROR	network error (see later)
86	ERROR_INVALID_PASSWORD	incorrect password for the remote resource
	ERROR_NO_NET_OR_BAD_PATH	cannot complete because the network client is not responding correctly or the remote resource path is wrong
	ERROR_NO_NETWORK	network has not been detected
	ERROR_SUCCESS	function completed correctly
	ERROR_DEVICE_IN_USE	device is in use by an active process and cannot be disconnected
	ERROR_NOT_CONNECTED	the named resource is not currently redirected or connected
	ERROR_OPEN_FILES	(only applies with bForce=FALSE) open files are in use over the connection

NOTE

All these error codes are defined in the API Viewer and should be copied and pasted as constants into your VB project.

Related Windows API functions

So far, I have covered the basic network API functions of Windows; however, there are a number of general API functions that are particularly useful and relevant to any network application. For example, you can use API functions to find out the version of Windows that is running; useful to check before you call one of the 32-bit API functions when running on an older version of Windows. You can also use APIs to find out where the Windows system files are located and so work out if this copy of Windows is shared from a network server or running on a local computer.

Getting the Windows version information

GetVersionEx(...)

```
LngReturnVal = GetVersionEx(VersionInfo)
```

This basic API call will return the version information about the copy of Windows that is currently running on the computer.

library   kernel32

parameters

parameter	*explanation*
VersionInfo	custom data structure that is used to store the Windows major and minor version numbers; has the following structure:

```
Type VersionInfo

    VersionInfoSize as Long     'size of information
    MajorVersion as Long        'major version number
    MinorVersion as Long        'minor version number
    BuildNumber as Long         'build number
    PlatformID as Long          'type of Windows (NT, 95, etc)
    VersionTxt as String * 128  'full text string of info

end Type
```

For example, to use this function to get the version information you could use the following code, which also defines the custom structure and the system DLL library that contains the function.

```
Private Type VersionInfo

    VersionInfoSize as Long    'size of information
    MajorVersion as Long       'major version number
    MinorVersion as Long       'minor version number
    BuildNumber as Long        'build number
    PlatformID as Long         'Platform identification
    VersionTxt as String * 128'full text string of info

end Type

Private Declare Function GetVersionEx Lib "kernel32" Alias
"GetVersionExA"(lpVersionInformation As VersionInfo) as Long

Private Sub Form_Load()

    Dim Version as VersionInfo
    ReportOut as String

    Version.VersionInfoSize = Len(Version)
    GetVersionEx Version
    if Version.PlatformID = 0 then ReportOut = "Windows 32bit"
    if Version.PlatformID = 1 then ReportOut = "Windows"
    if Version.PlatformID = 2 then ReportOut = "Windows NT"

    ReportOut=ReportOut + Version.MajorVersion +
    Version.MinorVersion + "Build:" + Version.BuildNumber

End Sub
```

Getting Windows directory information

There are four separate API functions that can be used to retrieve information about where the Windows files are located. They report on the directory location of the current directory, the \Windows directory, the \Windows\System directory and the Temp directory (I have used their usual names for convenience, but the directory names, as well as their locations, could be different).

The four API functions are GetCurrentDirectory(), GetWindowsDirectory(), GetSystemDirectory(), and GetTempPath(); they would be used as follows.

```
Private Declare Function GetCurrentDirectory Lib "kernel32" Alias
"GetCurrentDirectoryA" (ByVal lngBuffer as Long, ByVal strBuffer
as String) as Long
```

```
Private Declare Function GetWindowsDirectory Lib "kernel32" Alias
"GetWindowsDirectoryA" (ByVal strBuffer as String, ByVal lngBuffer
as Long) as Long

Private Declare Function GetSystemDirectory Lib "kernel32" Alias
"GetSystemDirectoryA" (ByVal strBuffer as String, ByVal lngBuffer
as Long) as Long

Private Declare Function GetTempPath Lib "kernel32" Alias
"GetTempPathA" (ByVal lngBuffer as Long, ByVal strBuffer as String)
as Long

    Private Sub Form_Load()

        Dim CurrentDir as String
        Dim WindowsDir as String
        Dim SystemDir as String
        Dim TempDir as String

        CurrentDir = Space(500)
        WindowsDir = Space(500)
        SystemDir = Space(500)
        TempDir = Space(500)

        'The functions return the size of text string,
        'so use Left() function to trim this down to size,
        'deleting any unwanted information

        CurrentDir = Left(CurrentDir, GetCurrentDirectory(Len(
            CurrentDir), CurrentDir))
        WindowsDir = Left(WindowsDir, GetCurrentWindowsDirectory(
            WindowsDir, Len(WindowsDir))
        SystemDir = Left(SystemDir, GetSystemDirectory(
            SystemDir,Len(SystemDir))
        TempDir = Left(TempDir, GetTempPath(Len(TempDir), TempDir)

    EndSub
```

Retrieving user and workstation information

Many of the functions that you will want to use require two pieces of information: the local computer name and the current user's name. For example, if you want to send email (see Chapter 5) using the MAPI functions, the username is required to define the user as the sender and to access the postoffice.

Windows 95 and NT both provide API functions that allow a developer to retrieve the stored computer name and the name of the current user of the computer. These two functions, GetComputerName() and GetUserName() are described below.

GetComputerName(...)

GetComputerName(strBuffer, nSize)

parameters	*parameter*	*explanation*
	strBuffer	string that will contain the name of the local computer, as defined in the Registry
	nSize	long pointer that contains the maximum number of characters to be copied into the strBuffer string; make sure that this is set to a big enough length or the function will fail if the name returned is longer than this limit

GetUserName(...)

GetUserName(strBuffer, nSize)

parameters	*parameter*	*explanation*
	strBuffer	string that will contain the name of the local computer, as defined in the Registry
	nSize	long pointer that contains the maximum number of characters to be copied into the strBuffer string; make sure that this is set to a big enough length or the function will fail if the name returned is longer than this limit

If you are building an admistrative front-end to Windows 95 or NT, you could also use the following function, SetComputerName(), to allow a user with administrative rights to set the local computer name. This function will change the name entry in the Registry and will take effect the next time that Windows starts up. The syntax for this command is given below.

SetComputerName(...)

SetComputerName(strBuffer)

parameters	*parameter*	*explanation*
	strBuffer	string that contains the new computer name—which must not be greater than MAX_COMPUTERNAME_LENGTH characters long

Conclusion

In this chapter, I have described the ways of using the standard Windows API functions that are available to any Windows application—if the developer digs deep enough. I have also included the basic functions that allow the developer to access a Microsoft network operating system (whether a simple Win95-based workgroup or NT server). All these functions allow you to leave the hard work of managing the network resources to Windows. The functions described in this chapter are the simplest set of commands to help you make the most of any network. If you want to delve deeper into an operating system, look to Chapter 4 in which I cover two of the main non-Microsoft network operating system standards: Novell NetWare and NetBIOS networks.

3

Using LAN Resources

Introduction

Windows supports resource sharing that allows a group of users to share drive or printer resources over a network with no effort—it's all managed by and hidden inside Windows. In the previous chapter, you saw how the basic Windows API could be used to access these resources; in this chapter I cover the ways in which you can detect, connect and use remote resources.

Logon and share security

Once you start to access shared resources available on a network, you need to understand how the various logon and validation processes work within Windows. The basic principles of Windows security are very straightforward and are explained in the following section of this chapter. Security within Windows NT server is taken to a new microscopic level and allows the server or an application to request authentication for a process, resource or communications channel. This level of security is controlled by a range of dozens of new APIs that are, unfortunately, out of the scope of this book—we will stick with Windows 95.

One of the reasons why the process is straightforward is because security under Windows 3.1*x* and 95 is simple. There are basically just two modes of operation—user-level security, which is controlled by a central server that requires a valid username and password; and share-level security in which each resource is assigned its own password. These features are all available from VB; to make life easier for the user, Windows 95 includes a password caching feature that records (in encrypted form) the passwords to servers and resources.

Once you have installed your network components, you can start to configure them so that the user security system is working correctly.

From the Control Panel/Networks icon you can define the way in which the user logs into a server (if at all) and the type of security that external users will be faced with when attempting to share a local resource.

Figure 3.1:
*User valida-
tion can be
configured to
use a central
NT server.*

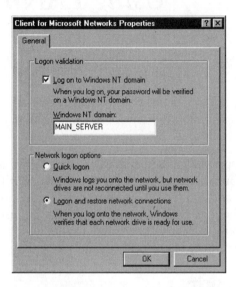

User validation

The first of the options in a Microsoft client is the ability to log on to a Windows NT domain using your username and password. You don't have to select this option, even if you are connecting to an NT server; however, it gives you far better control over the network's management if you do have an NT domain name server. If you do select this option, enter the name of the domain (or the relevant server) in the panel below.

It might be easier to not bother selecting that your user is checked by the domain server, but if the logon is not validated by the domain server, no connections will be made and any login scripts that you have set up will not be run.

Below the domain name check are two choices defining how Windows will connect you to the network: either a quick connect or a verify connect. The default setting for this is Quick Connect.

Quick Connect   When selected, Windows will automatically try to log you in to every resource you have specified.

Verify Connect   When this option is selected, Windows
                        will check to see if the resource is available
                        before trying to log you in to that resource.

Figure 3.2:
Windows 95
supports
persistent
connections
that ensure
resource
reconnection.

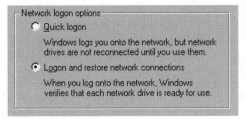

Unless you're not confident that all your normal connections are available, it's far easier and quicker to select Quick Connect. If you chop and change between resources, or if you rely on a peer-shared resource, you might want to ensure that it's there before trying to log in to it.

TIP

If you are having problems getting validation from a domain server, check that you can actually make a connection by opening an MS-DOS session and entering the NET USE command. If you cannot even make a connection, then you either do not have full access to the domain server or you have the wrong server name.

Primary network logon

If you have installed more than one client component, you can define the client that will be used as the primary shell when carrying out a logon. For example, if you have a local Novell NetWare server that's used for all your everyday file storage, and a main NT server that's used for occasional file sharing, you would install two clients and set the NetWare client as the primary network logon.

Workstation identification

The second page within the Control Panel/Network icon is labeled Identification. This page lets you enter the name of the computer, the name of the workgroup it belongs to, and a line that can describe the computer or include simple notes. To view the existing settings for the computer, click on the Identification page tag of the Network icon in the Control Panel.

The **Computer name** can be any name, up to 15 characters long. This name must be a unique entry on the network and cannot include spaces. A good way of naming your computers is to give them a name based on their department, office or floor together with a number. For example, ACCOUNTS1, ACCOUNTS2, and so on for the PCs in the accounts department, and ORDER1, ORDER2, for the PCs in the order-processing department. It's not a very good idea to set the computer name to the user's name or to the name of the PC's manufacturer. For example, if you call the first PC "SIMON", this doesn't help you work out where it is, nor allow for another PC owned by a Simon.

The **Workgroup name** has similar limitations to the Computer name setting—only 15 characters long and no spaces. It does not have to be unique, or you would only have one user per workgroup! Try to define workgroups that embrace a number of users within an office or using a particular server or resource. If the PC is already connected to a network, it will have detected any existing workgroups; you can scroll through the list by clicking on the down arrow beside the Workgroup entry line. If you type in a name that does not exist, you are creating a new workgroup.

Lastly, the **Computer Description** lets you enter a descriptive line for this particular computer. This line is displayed beside the computer when other users are browsing through the network using Network Neighborhood or a similar utility.

Figure 3.3:
Each worksta-tion can have identifying fields that can be accessed from a VB *application.*

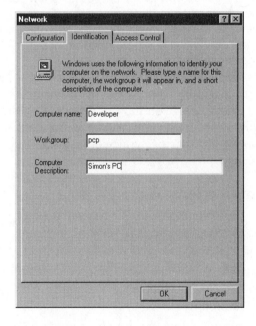

Controlling access to the workstation resources

The third page tag in the Network settings window is labeled Access Control and lets you define, in broad terms, whether you want to implement share-level or user-level security when sharing local resources. You can block this altogether by not sharing any local resources, but then a lot of the extra functionality that Windows 95 brings to the network would be lost.

If you define a share-level form of security this means that each separate resource has its own access control definitions: a user SIMON might be allowed full access to a particular file but can only print from a shared printer if he enters the correct password. This printer password could be different from the password required to access a local folder. In short, share-level security is very flexible and allows each user to tailor their security according to each local resource.

Figure 3.4:
Selecting
share-level
access control
allows you to
assign pass-
words to
shared
resources.

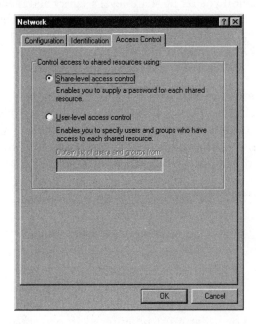

User-level security takes a different approach. In order to be able to use any particular local resource, a user must enter the correct password and so "login" to the local PC. Once logged in, the user can then use any resource he or she is allowed to. The owner of the local resource can prevent users seeing particular folders or using resources and even attach extra passwords to certain resources. The supervisor can define the individual users that can have access to the workstation either by user or by group. Unfortunately, Windows 95 isn't very good at storing this security information and so it relies on another server to validate users and groups, for example a Windows NT server.

In general, if the network is a small local system connecting just a few users, you will probably not bother too much with security and so share-level access control is the most flexible. However, if you are a manager of a larger network you will soon find the mass of extra passwords and security levels confusing to both users and supervisors. If each users sets up several different passwords, no one will ever remember any of them or, worse, write them down, and the point of the security will be lost. To select either type of access control, click the relevant radio button. In the case of user-level security, you will also need to specify the name of the server or NT domain controller that will validate the user and group names.

NOTE

Watch out if you set up share-level security and then decide to try out user-level security—you'll lose all your share settings when you make the switch, so make sure that you backup the registry files, USER.DAT and SYSTEM.DAT, beforehand.

Share-level security

Share-level security is the only type of security available for peer-to-peer networks built using only Windows 95 or Windows for Workgroups. If you have a central server running Windows NT or Novell NetWare then you also have the option to support user-level security.

Figure 3.5:
Share-level
security
settings for
basic
operations.

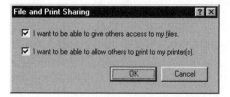

Share-level security relies on the owner of a shared resource specifying a password that must be entered in order for another user to be allowed to use the resource.

NOTE

If you are using a computer that is running the Microsoft File and Printer Sharing for NetWare, this PC cannot support share-level security—you can only implement user-level security on this PC, even though it will be sharing local resources.

User-level security

User-level security relies on a list of users or groups and their respective passwords and rights. This list is stored on a server, not on a local Windows 95 computer. The server would be running either Windows NT or Novell NetWare. Users, groups and their access rights are created and edited using the respective tools of the server's operating system: for example, in NetWare 3.*x* you would use SYSCON and in NetWare 4.*x* you would use NWADMIN to create and administer users. Once you have created your users for the network, Windows 95 computers can then access this list and you can assign users various rights.

Password security

Access to the computer running Windows 95 and to the other resources on the network depends on the user typing in the correct password. Windows 95 includes a number of features that make it easier to enter passwords—but no easier to log in if you don't know the password!

When you use your computer on the network there are a number of different security levels that you have to pass through in order to gain access to the shared resources. First, you need to log on to the computer running Windows 95; if you are using user-level security you will also have to log on to a central server, which can then validate your name and password. Lastly, you will have to enter passwords to use various shared resources on the network. As you can see, there are a lot of passwords to enter, which would tempt a user to enter a simple or short password.

Figure 3.6:
*Two sets
of password
lists are
maintained
and can be
changed.*

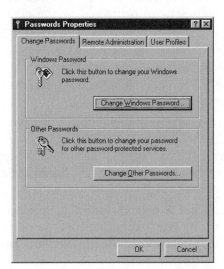

Windows gets around this problem with its unified logon feature. If you have the same password to log on to Windows 95 on your computer as the password required to log on to your main server, Windows will unify the two and log you in automatically. The flip side is that you can also prevent users from using Windows 95 if they don't know either their Windows password or their main server password (this is done through System Policies).

Another way in which Windows helps to minimize the number of passwords that need to be entered is when using share-level resources. The passwords to gain access to the shared resources can be stored (or cached) in a password file on your local computer. When you first connect to a shared resource, the password file records the path to the resource and the password. The next time you log in on your computer, the password file is unlocked by your main Windows 95 password and the connections re-established with Windows automatically sending the correct passwords.

You can turn off this password caching feature if you want to ensure that security is tightened. Alternatively, as the system supervisor you can also use the Password List Editor to view the contents of the password cache file.

Password caching

Windows 95, as described above, solves one of the problems of share-level security using password caching. Passwords for shared resources, together with the full path to the resource, are stored in a password list, given a PWL extension. The PWL file is stored on the local computer and is, naturally, password protected by the main Windows 95 password.

The PWL list contains the paths and passwords to any share-level resources you have connected to, any Windows NT servers that are not the primary logon server, or any NetWare servers that are not the preferred logon server.

When you first start Windows 95, the password caching feature is automatically enabled. When you first access a shared resource, a dialog box asking for the password is displayed. When you enter the password, make sure that you also check the Save the Password to list check box and your password will be saved in the PWL file.

If you do not want to provide automatic password caching, you can disable the feature by starting the System Policy Editor and selecting the Local Computer icon; now choose the Network properties branch and select Passwords—from this check the Disable Password Caching feature.

Password List Editor

If you ever have problems with the password list, or if you want to remove old or unused resource entries, you can edit the list using the Password List Editor. This displays the resources—but not their passwords—and lets you delete any selected.

Figure 3.7:
The Password List Editor allows a user to manage passwords.

To start the Password List Editor, select *Start ▸ Run* and enter the PWLEDIT name. If you have not already installed the PWLEDIT utility, you can do so by running the Add/Remove Programs icon from Control Panel and selecting the Have Disk button and entering the path \ADMIN\APPTOOLS\PWLEDIT to the CD-ROM distribution disc.

Logging on to the network

The first step before you can use or share any resource on the network is to log on to the network. There are two totally distinct ways in which this occurs, which depend on the type of access control (the security) that you have implemented for the network. There are, in addition to the access control levels, two levels at which you can log on to the network. These multiple levels do tend to make the subject of logging on the network rather confusing, not helped by the fact that out of the four levels, only two actually log you on to a network!

There are two levels of logon on either Microsoft or NetWare networks. These allow you to either log on to Windows 95 using a username and password or log on to a NetWare server or NT domain controller that validates your name and password.

The very first time that you start Windows 95 the user will be faced with a network login for each of the standalone servers (for example, a NetWare or NT server), plus a separate logon screen for Windows 95. If you make each password and username the same, the Windows 95 logon screen does not appear again. For example, if your network consists of a NetWare server and a small Windows 95 workgroup, you will have to enter logon details for the NetWare server and for Windows 95.

When you log in to Windows 95 you type in a username and a password. This information is used to recall any User Profiles and to access the password database that stores the passwords for the other servers you are connected to. If the user is not recognized, it is assumed to be a new user.

If your workstation is connected to a NetWare or NT server you will also have to enter your registered username and password that can then be validated on the server; you will also have to enter the domain controller name (for NT) or the preferred server name (for NetWare) of the server that will carry out the validation.

NOTE

The second and subsequent times that Windows is started, it will display the username and validating server name, leaving the user to enter the password; if the user is a new user, he will have to enter his new name and password.

Supervisor options

There is only one major change that a supervisor can put into practice, and this is to use System Policies. This is the only way to stop a user from logging on to both a server and Windows 95. On a standard setup, with no policies, any user can log into Windows 95 and use the applications; he will only be able to log into the validating server if he has the correct password.

By using System Policies, the supervisor can, to a certain degree, limit unauthorized access. If a user does not enter the correct password for Windows 95 he will not get access to the local resources. However, it's not difficult to get around System Policies: a user need only boot up from a local floppy disk to have full access.

Figure 3.8:
*System policy
to force logon
to a central NT
server.*

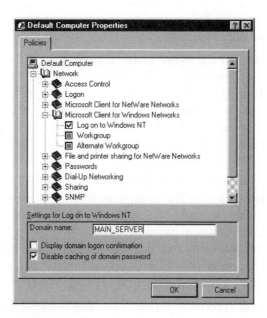

Browsing the network

Browsing the network allows you to view the resources available to
Windows from within your VB application. This is integrated so cleanly
that there will never be any problems with this process, but you might
occasionally see some oddities on the list of network resources as users
log on and off the network. You should read this section to understand
how browsing works before you make any assumptions about the
resources available on the network.

How network browsing works

The range of Windows operating systems (Windows NT, Windows for
Workgroups and Windows 95) all use a similar method for browsing
network resources that tries to minimize network traffic and keep
access time as low as possible, while working well on both small and
large networks.

The system works using the concept of a master browse server
(together with a backup browse server). For any one workgroup and
for each protocol used in the workgroup there is one master browse
server.

The master browse server maintains a master list of workgroups,
domains and computers in the workgroup. If a workgroup grows larger

than a dozen or 15 computers, the backup browse server will start to take a role in off-loading some of the workload on the master server.

How to set up a master browse server

The simplest method is to do nothing! When you first fire up Windows 95, it will check on the network to see if a master browse server already exists for the workgroup. If it cannot find one, then an automatic election takes place between the computers and one is elected as the master browse server. Similarly, an automatic process will allocate one of the PCs as a backup server (there can be more than one backup server per workgroup, depending on the size of the workgroup).

The allocation of the computer that is the master browse server is dynamic. For example, if you think that the browse list has been corrupted and users are having trouble in connecting to resources, you could shut down the PC that's operating as the master browse server and another will take its place. To see the current list of browse objects, the simplest command is to enter NET VIEW at the DOS command line.

Adding and removing items from the browse list

It's important to realize how new computers are added and old ones removed from a master browse list. The main point is that it is not an instant process. When a computer in a workgroup is switched on, it transmits its name and details to the master browse server. The master browse server updates its list and notifies the backup server that there is a new list available. The backup server updates its list and it is only then that the new computer would appear on a user's browse list or Network Neighborhood folder. The time delay can be as long as 15 minutes before the backup browse server receives the new updates, which is when the new computer finally appears on the users' screens.

When you shut down and switch off a PC, the reverse happens and the workstation tells the master browse server that it is no longer available. Again, the master server tells the backup server that an update is available and when the backup server is up to date the workstation will be removed from a user's list. If a workstation is not shut down properly—i.e., it's just switched off—then the whole process takes far longer. Because a workstation does not tell the master browse server it is no longer available, the master server must work this out for itself. As a result, the computer name could still appear on lists for up to 45 minutes after it's been switched off.

TIP

You can, as an administrator, limit the workgroups that a user can browse. This information is contained in the WRKGRP.INI file.

Programming for network drives

The simplest way of viewing all the local and mapped network drives on a computer is to use the standard VB drive list control. This drop-down combo-box lists all active mappings without any extra programming effort and provides a good way of keeping track of your current drive mappings. With this in mind, the following section shows you how to connect to a remote shared resource and map the resource to a local drive name; in some cases you will be prompted for a password (if the user has selected share-level security).

Connecting to a network drive

To connect to a network drive under 16-bit Windows, you should use the WNetAddConnection() API function (see Chapter 2 for details on all network APIs). This API call takes three parameters: the full path to the remote drive, the password, and the local drive letter to be mapped.

Figure 3.9:
A simple form
that allows a
user to select
and connect
to a network
shared folder.

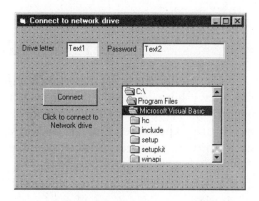

In the following code, the Connect button does all the work when clicked by the user. It takes the full UNC path to the remote resource from the edit box on the form (together with the password and the local drive letter). It then calls the API and, if the call was a success, refreshes the drive listing box to reflect the new mapping.

```
Sub Connect_click()

    Dim Succeed As Long
    Dim fullUNC As String, Password As String, localDrive As String

    fullUNC = EnterUNC.Text
    Password = EnterPassword.Text
    localDrive = EnterDrive.Text
```

```
Succeed = WNetAddConnection(fullUNC, Password, localDrive)
if Succeed <> ERROR_SUCCESS Then
   MsgBox "Error connecting"
Else
   Drive1.Refresh
End If

End Sub
```

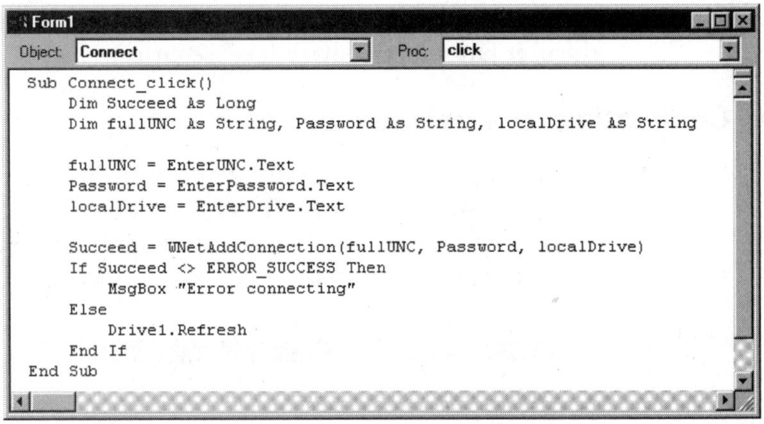

Figure 3.10:
*The program
linked to the
Connect
button of the
previous form.*

```
Form1
Object: Connect                        Proc: click

Sub Connect_click()
    Dim Succeed As Long
    Dim fullUNC As String, Password As String, localDrive As String

    fullUNC = EnterUNC.Text
    Password = EnterPassword.Text
    localDrive = EnterDrive.Text

    Succeed = WNetAddConnection(fullUNC, Password, localDrive)
    If Succeed <> ERROR_SUCCESS Then
        MsgBox "Error connecting"
    Else
        Drive1.Refresh
    End If
End Sub
```

You should try to make the error reporting a little friendlier than the basic version I have here. A good error trap would be to detect the wrong password and prompt for a new password. The error constants for this function are all described on page 73 and should be copied as a set of constants into your project file—an invalid password is reported as ERROR_INVALID_PASSWORD, code 86&.

The WNetAddConnection() API function will work fine, but it is only worth using if you are developing for a 16-bit platform. For 32-bit Windows development, try to use WNetAddConnection2(), which is an improved function call. This uses a different set of parameters—primarily in that it uses a NETRESOURCE object to hold all the network connection details. The same routine as above can be modified to work with WNetAddConnection2() as shown below:

```
Sub Connect2_click()

    Dim Succeed As Long
    Dim Password As String, User As String
    Dim Connection As NETRESOURCE

    Connection.lngType = RESOURCETYPE_DISK
    Connection.strLocalName = EnterDrive.Text
```

```
Connection.strRemoteName = EnterUNC.Text
Connection.strProvider = ""
Password = EnterPassword.Text
User = ""

Succeed = WNetAddConnection2(Connection, Password, User, 0)

if Succeed <> ERROR_SUCCESS Then
    MsgBox "Error connecting"
Else
    Drive1.Refresh
End If

End Sub
```

Figure 3.11:
Connecting to
a shared folder
using the
32-bit API call.

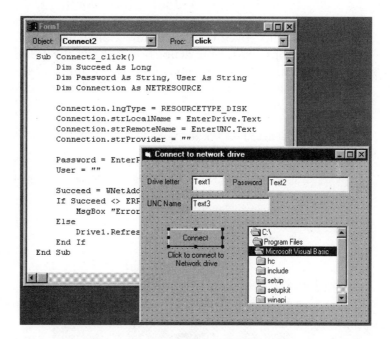

The Connection variable is derived from the NETRESOURCE structure and contains all the main details that were previously supplied as command-line parameters to the function call. With this function, you are able to define if you want to set the new mapping as a persistent connection—in which case it will be written to the user's Profile file (see Chapter 1 for more on Profiles). In this example, I want a session-only connection so have set the last parameter to zero. To define this new mapping as a persistent connection, the function call would look like:

```
Succeed = WNetAddConnection2(Connection, Password, User,
        CONNECT_UPDATE_PROFILE)
```

Note that the two constants that I have used in these examples are derived from the API declaration and should be added to your project's constant declaration page together with the function declarations and the system libraries for the function. The start of your project code should look like this:

```
Public Const CONNECT_UPDATE_PROFILE = &H1
Public Const RESOURCE_TYPE_DISK = &H1
Public Const ERROR_SUCCESS = 0&
Private Declare Function WNetAddConnection Lib "MPRLIB" (ByVal
strResourceName As String, strPassword As String, strLocalName
As String)
```

If you want to avoid using these constants, drive strings and UNC paths within your application, you can turn to the predefined dialog box called by the WNetConnectionDialog() function. When called, this pops up a simple dialog box that asks the user the same questions as our examples shown above. The next simple utility has a Connect button that calls the WNetConnectionDialog() function to do the work of mapping a drive.

```
Sub Connect1_Click()

    Dim Succeed As Long
    Succeed = WNetConnectionDialog(hWnd, RESOURCETYPE_DISK)
    if Succeed <> ERROR_SUCCESS Then
        MsgBox "Canceled"
    Else
        Drive1.Refresh
    End If

End Sub
```

Figure 3.12:
The dialog box
displayed to
connect to a
resource.

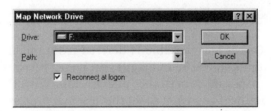

To complement this dialog box, let's add another command button to call the second system dialog box to allow a user to disconnect (un-map) a drive. This dialog displays a list of the existing mappings and allows a user to highlight a mapped drive from the list and disconnect the local drive mapped to this resource.

```
Sub Disconnect1_Click()

    Dim Succeed As Long

    Succeed = WNetDisconnectDialog(hWnd, RESOURCETYPE_DISK)

    if Succeed <> ERROR_SUCCESS Then
        MsgBox "Canceled"
    Else
        Drive1.Refresh
    End If

End Sub
```

Figure 3.13:
*The matching
disconnect
dialog box.*

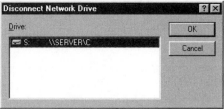

Reporting mapped drive information

Once you have mapped a local drive to a remote resource, it can be useful to view the system information about the mapping; if you are sharing a local resource, it is just as useful to know which other user on the
system is currently using your resource. Two more WNet API calls carry
out each of these functions. In the following utility, there is an edit box
(resourceName) into which the user can type in the name of the local
resource (such as F:). There's also a command button—Query1—that
will call the function and display the mapped path to the resource in the
second edit box, resourceUNC.

```
Sub Query1_Click()
    'To view the full path mapped to a resource
    Dim fullPath As String
    Dim lngFullPath As Long
    Dim Resource As String
    Dim Succeed As Long
    fullPath = Space(100)
    lngFullPath = len(fullPath)
    Resource = resourceName.Text
    Succeed = WNetGetConnection(Resource, fullPath, lngFullPath)
    resourceUNC.Text = fullPath

End Sub
```

Figure 3.14:
*Our simple
program to
display the
UNC of a
resource.*

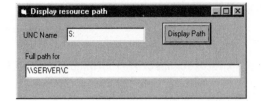

With just a couple of changes, we can turn this little routine into a call to WNetGetUser() that will return the name of the user who is currently using the device.

```
Sub Query1_Click()          'To view the user of a resource

    Dim User As String
    Dim lngUser As Long
    Dim Resource As String
    Dim Succeed As Long

    User = Space(100)
    lngUser = len(fullPath)
    Resource = resourceName.Text

    Succeed = WNetGetUser(Resource, User, lngUser)
    resourceUser.Text = User

End Sub
```

Figure 3.15:
*The earlier
UNC form
modified to
show the user.*

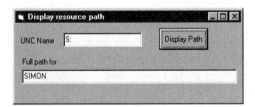

Using network printers

Printers can be easily shared between a group of users and all the data transfer and control is managed invisibly by Windows. Just as with the network drive resource described above, you can control and access a shared network printer (or share a local printer) using the range of WNet API functions that are described in detail in Chapter 2.

Sharing a printer

Making a local printer shareable to other users on the network is very much the same process as sharing a drive resource. The printer definitions for your local printer are stored in the Printers folder of the MyComputer icon. To share a printer, you need to access its Properties sheet and change settings to determine who can use the printer.

One point to bear in mind, which might sound odd, is that you can only share a local printer. For example, if your Printers folder contains icons for a local printer, a NetWare server-based print queue and a shared network printer, then the only printer that you can share with other users is the local printer.

For example, in the case of the NetWare print queue you might want to try and share this with a user who does not have rights to directly access the queue—you cannot.

Share-level printer controls

If you are using share-level security, you'll see only one field that allows you to enter a password for full access to the printer—there's no point having anything other than full access to a printer, unlike a drive.

User-level printer controls

For networks running user-level security, there is a larger window at the bottom of the Sharing page tag that lists all the users or groups that can access the printer. To add a user or group to the list, select the Add button you can then choose from a list of users.

Programming for network printers

Working with a shared network printer follows nearly identical steps and function calls as described in the section above dealing with network drives. The API functions are called with a different resource identifier to tell Windows that you want to handle a printer rather than a drive resource. I will start this section by covering the basics—in fact, similar ground to drive resource mapping—and then moving on to micro printer controls rather than these macro-level printer mapping controls.

Connecting to a network printer

To connect to a network printer on a 16-bit Windows platform, you should use the WNetAddConnection() API function (see Chapter 2 for details on all network APIs). This API call takes three parameters: the full path to the remote printer, any password required for the printer, and the local printer port to be mapped.

In the following code, the Connect button does all the work when clicked by the user. It takes the full path to the remote printer resource from the edit box on the form (together with the password and the local printer port). The program then calls the API and, if the call was a success, refreshes the printer listing box to reflect the new mapping.

```
Sub Connect_click()

    Dim Succeed As Long
    Dim fullUNC As String, Password As String, localPort As String

    fullUNC = EnterUNC.Text
    Password = EnterPassword.Text
    localPort = EnterPort.Text

    Succeed = WNetAddConnection(fullUNC, Password, localPort)
    if Succeed <> ERROR_SUCCESS Then
        MsgBox "Error connecting"
    End If

End Sub
```

As in the earlier drive example, it is worth adding a user-friendly error trap to this example using the error codes listed on page 73.

For 32-bit Windows development, you should try to use the improved WNetAddConnection2() function call. This uses a different set of parameters—primarily in that it uses a NETRESOURCE object to hold all the network connection details. The same routine as above can be modified to work with WNetAddConnection2() as shown below:

```
Sub Connect2_click()

    Dim Succeed As Long
    Dim Password As String, User As String
    Dim Connection As NETRESOURCE

    Connection.lngType = RESOURCETYPE_PRINT
    Connection.strLocalName = EnterPort.Text
    Connection.strRemoteName = EnterUNC.Text
    Connection.strProvider = ""

    Password = EnterPassword.Text
    User = ""
```

```
Succeed = WNetAddConnection2(Connection, Password, User, 0)
if Succeed <> ERROR_SUCCESS Then
   MsgBox "Error connecting"
End If

End Sub
```

The `Connection` variable is derived from the `NETRESOURCE` structure and contains all the main details that were previously supplied as command-line parameters to the function call. With this function, you are able to define if you want to set the new mapping as a persistent connection, in which case it will be written to the user's Profile file (see Chapter 1 for more on Profiles). In this example, I want a session-only connection so have set the last parameter to zero. If I wanted to define this new mapping as a persistent connection, the function call would look like this:

```
Succeed = WNetAddConnection2(Connection, Password, User,
       CONNECT_UPDATE_PROFILE)
```

Note that the constants that I have used in these examples are slightly different from those used in the drive mapping examples earlier in this chapter. As before, you should add these constants to your project's constant declaration page together with the function declarations and the system libraries for the function. The start of your project code should look like this:

```
Public Const CONNECT_UPDATE_PROFILE = &H1
Public Const RESOURCE_TYPE_PRINT = &H2
Public Const ERROR_SUCCESS = 0&
Private Declare Function WNetAddConnection Lib "MPRLIB" (ByVal
strResourceName As String, strPassword As String, strLocalName
As String)
```

The predefined dialog box used in mapping drives can also be used to map printers using the WNetConnectionDialog() function.

```
Sub Connect1_Click()

   'example of the system dialog box to map a printer
   Dim Succeed As Long
   Succeed = WNetConnectionDialog(hWnd, RESOURCETYPE_PRINT)
   if Succeed <> ERROR_SUCCESS Then
      MsgBox "Canceled"
   End If

End Sub
```

Figure 3.16:
The system dialog box to capture a printer port.

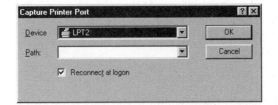

To complement this dialog box, we can again add a command button as we did with the drive mapping example to call the second system dialog box to allow a user to disconnect (unmap) a printer. This dialog displays a list of the existing mappings and allows a user to highlight a mapped printer from the list and disconnect the local printer port mapped to this resource.

```
Sub Disconnect1_Click()

    Dim Succeed As Long
    Succeed = WNetDisconnectDialog(hWnd, RESOURCETYPE_PRINT)
    if Succeed <> ERROR_SUCCESS Then
        MsgBox "Canceled"
    End If

End Sub
```

Figure 3.17:
The system dialog box to end a printer capture.

Reporting mapped printer information

The reporting API functions we used earlier in this chapter are just as happy reporting back information about a mapped printer as reporting about a mapped drive. In the following utility, there is an edit box (resourceName) into which the user can type in the name of the local resource (such as LPT1). There's also a command button—Query1— that will call the function and display the mapped path to the resource in the second edit box, resourceUNC.

```
Sub Query1_Click()

    'To view the full path mapped to a resource

    Dim fullPath As String
    Dim lngFullPath As Long
    Dim Resource As String
    Dim Succeed As Long

    fullPath = Space(100)
    lngFullPath = len(fullPath)
    Resource = resourceName.Text

    Succeed = WNetGetConnection(Resource, fullPath, lngFullPath)
    resourceUNC.Text = fullPath

End Sub
```

Figure 3.18:
Our earlier
code modified
to work with a
printer instead
of a folder.

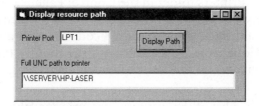

With just a couple of changes, we can turn this little routine into a call to WNetGetUser() that will return the name of the user who is currently using the device.

```
Sub Query1_Click()

    'To view the user of a resource

    Dim User As String
    Dim lngUser As Long
    Dim Resource As String
    Dim Succeed As Long

    User = Space(100)
    lngUser = len(fullPath)
    Resource = resourceName.Text

    Succeed = WNetGetUser(Resource, User, lngUser)
    resourceUser.Text = User

End Sub
```

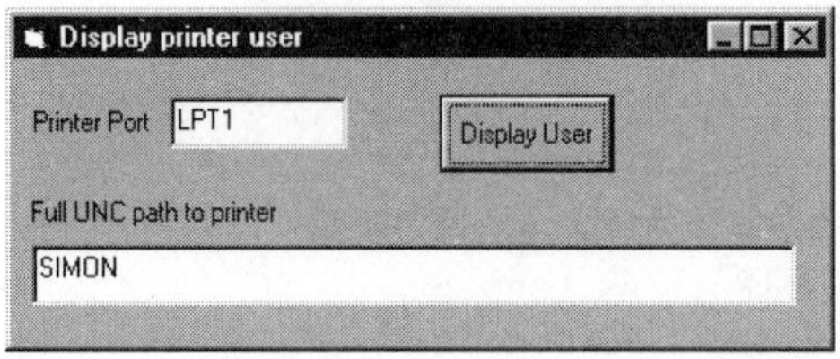

Figure 3.19:
*The code
modified once
more to show
the user.*

If you flip back a couple of pages, you might notice that these two examples are exactly the same as the previous utilities that reported on drive mapping and users—not a line of code has changed! The only difference is that the user enters a different local resource name.

The Printers Collection

The Printers Collection is a Windows system object that contains a list of all the printers currently installed and available to a user or application under Windows. If you want to see a list of these printers, take a look at the Printers folder in the Control Panel. Some of these printers will be network printers, others local or fax modems. It is important to note that although you can use VB code to select any printer from the Printers Collection, you cannot add or modify the entries from VB code—you must do this via the Control Panel (or the installation/setup utilities).

To build a list of the printers currently available on your computer, use the following code:

```
Sub List1_Click()

    Dim listPrinter As Printer
        For each listPrinter in Printers
            ListBox.Add listPrinter.DeviceName
        Next

End Sub
```

Notice that the first line of the routine uses a structure called `Printers`. This object can be used to create a print image in memory before it is printed, but this is not always the best way to print, since it requires numerous lines of code. However, the Printers object does provide basic information about the printers in the Printers Collection. We have already displayed the name of each printer in the collection using the `Printers.DeviceName` element, but there is also the `Port` element to the object that is useful in identifying the local printers or mapped network printers.

Error handling for network API calls

Table 3.1 *Standard error codes returned by functions*

Constant	Code	Meaning
5&	ERROR_ACCESS_DENIED	access to network resource denied
85	ERROR_ALREADY_ASSIGNED	network resource is already connected
	ERROR_BAD_DEV_TYPE	local device and network device do not match
	ERROR_BAD_DEVICE	incorrect resource name in strLocalName
67	ERROR_BAD_NET_NAME	incorrect resource name in strResourceName
1206	ERROR_BAD_PROFILE	User Profile is incorrect for this connection
	ERROR_BUSY	provider busy so a new connection cannot be made
	ERROR_CANCELLED	attempt to create a connection was cancelled, either by the user, the provider or for another reason
	ERROR_CANNOT_OPEN_PROFILE	Windows cannot open the User Profile for a persistent connection
	ERROR_DEVICE_ALREADY_REMEMBERED	the User Profile already has an entry for this strLocalName device
1208	ERROR_EXTENDED_ERROR	network error
86	ERROR_INVALID_PASSWORD	incorrect password for the remote resource
	ERROR_NO_NET_OR_BAD_PATH	cannot complete because the network client is not responding correctly or the remote resource path is wrong
	ERROR_NO_NETWORK	network has not been detected
	ERROR_SUCCESS	function completed correctly
	ERROR_DEVICE_IN_USE	device is in use by an active process and cannot be disconnected
	ERROR_NOT_CONNECTED	the named resource is not currently redirected or connected
	ERROR_OPEN_FILES	(only applies with bForce=FALSE) open files are in use over the connection

The network API calls used in this chapter and described in Chapter 2 all return a set of error codes. These are listed in the Text API Viewer utility, but you should make sure that you have included the error codes and an error handler in your network applications.

Error handler

The basis of the network error handler is best created as a way of testing for the successful completion of a network function. All of the network API functions will return the ERROR_SUCCESS (=0&) value if they have completed successfully, or an error code if there has been a problem. When calling a function, pass its result directly to a error-handling routine to test for success or a problem.

The error handler would first test the return value from the function to see if it completed successfully. If it has not, it can then use a Select-Case structure to convert the error code to a text message that is returned to the original network routine.

For example, the following subroutine could be used to check the value returned from any of the WNet functions described in Chapter 2.

```
Function ErrorSuccess(TestCode As Long, TextMsg As String) As
Boolean

    'If the function had no error, return False

    If TestCode = ERROR_SUCCESS Then
        ErrorSuccess = False
    Else
        ErrorSuccess = True
        Select Case TestCode
            'Enter your own descriptions for each error, or
            'process accordingly
            Case ERROR_ACCESS_DENIED:
            Case ERROR_ALREADY_ASSIGNED:
            Case ERROR_BAD_DEV_TYPE:
            Case ERROR_BAD_DEVICE:
            Case ERROR_BAD_NET_NAME:
            Case ERROR_BAD_PROFILE:
            Case ERROR_BUSY:
            Case ERROR_CANCELLED:
            Case ERROR_CANNOT_OPEN_PROFILE:
            Case ERROR_DEVICE_ALREADY_REMEMBERED:
            Case ERROR_INVALID_PASSWORD:
            Case ERROR_NO_NET_OR_BAD_PATH:
            Case ERROR_NO_NETWORK:
            Case ERROR_SUCCESS:
            Case ERROR_DEVICE_IN_USE:
```

```
                    Case ERROR_NOT_CONNECTED:
                    Case ERROR_OPEN_FILES:
                        'The exception is an extended error, which is passed
                        'to the ExtendedError() function for decoding using
                        'an API call
                    Case ERROR_EXTENDED_ERROR:
                    ExtendedError()
                    Case Else:
                End Select

End Function
```

The following function is used to manage and decode any extended error messages supplied directly from the network provider (the network operating system). It uses another API call to request the full text message relating to the extended error.

```
Function ExtendedError() As String

'This function requests the full network error code and
'message from the provider

    Dim strError As String
    Dim ErrorVal As Long              'error value
    Dim ErrorCode As Long             'error code
    Dim ErrorDes As String            'error description
    Dim ErrorDesLng As Long           'length of description
    Dim ErrorProvider As String       'network provider name
    Dim ErrorProviderLng As Long      'length of network provider name

    ErrorDes = Space(256)
    ErrorDesLng = Len(ErrorDes)
    ErrorProvider = Space(30)
    ErrorProviderLng = Len(ErrorProvider)
    ErrorVal = WNetGetLastError(ErrorCode, ErrorDes, ErrorDesLng,
        ErrorProvider, ErrorProviderLng)

    If ErrorVal = ERROR_SUCCESS Then
        strError = "Error description:" & ErrorDes & "Code:" &
        ErrorCode & "From network Provider:" & ErrorProvider
    Else
        strError = "Cannot Process Error"
    End If

    ExtendedError = strError

End Function
```

This error reporting could be used directly each time you access a network API function to check the results before continuing. For example, taking one of our earlier routines to modify it for the error reporting:

```
Sub Connect_click()

    Dim Succeed As Long
    Dim fullUNC As String, Password As String, localPort As String
    Dim ErrorMsg As String

    fullUNC = EnterUNC.Text
    Password = EnterPassword.Text
    localPort = EnterPort.Text

    Succeed = WNetAddConnection(fullUNC, Password, localPort)
    if ErrorSuccess(Succeed, ErrorMsg) Then
    MsgBox ErrorMsg
    End If

End Sub
```

This type of error reporting and extended error reporting should be a standard part of all your VB network applications. Add it along with the constant declarations to all your projects for better error handling!

Conclusion

This chapter has shown you how to support simple network access to a shared resource in two different ways—either using the API functions to configure and then execute a call or calling a standard system dialog box that allows the user to select a resource. If you want complete control, program the APIs in code; if you want a user interface, use the system dialogs.

4

Programming NetWare and NetBIOS

Introduction

The programming examples that I have described in Chapter 2 cover generic network functions that will work with any Windows-compatible network operating system. In all the cases, it is Windows that carries out the low-level calls to the network client shell, protecting the user from the worst of assembly-language routines.

In Chapter 3, I also described a number of functions that are specific to the Microsoft LAN Manager/Windows NTAS network operating system. These are useful when requesting information about domain names and user groups—both LAN Manager-specific features. However, the world has more network operating systems than just Microsoft software!

In this chapter, I cover the ways of programming for the Novell NetWare network operating system and NetBIOS protocols. The NetWare environment has a very rich set of functions that can be used with or instead of the generic Windows network functions described in Chapter 2.

Developing for Novell NetWare

The Novell NetWare network operating system (NOS) is a very powerful application that provides file and print sharing, client–server platform support and one of the best global naming services around. For basic network functionality with NetWare, you can use the generic network functions described in Chapter 2. However, NetWare has a very rich set of function calls—far more sophisticated and varied than those supplied by the LAN Manager NOS. The problem for VB developers is that NetWare calls are not featured as part of the Windows client operating system, so it takes a little extra effort to deal with this NOS.

If you do want to handle NetWare functions from within VB, you will need the NWCALLS.DLL library that is supplied by Novell (available from the ftp.novell.com site or from CompuServe). This carries out the low-level interrupt calls that drive the workstation client and give a user application access to the network operating system features such as user details, bindery functions and more.

When dealing with NetWare, the main problem is that although the hundreds of network functions are well documented, and a DLL is supplied, there are few native resources available for Visual Basic. A number of third-party developers have produced VBX and OCX/ActiveX components that take the sting out of NetWare interrupt calls; a good example is the Apiary control (www.apiary.com).

Figure 4.1:
Apiary supplies a range of components to access NetWare functions.

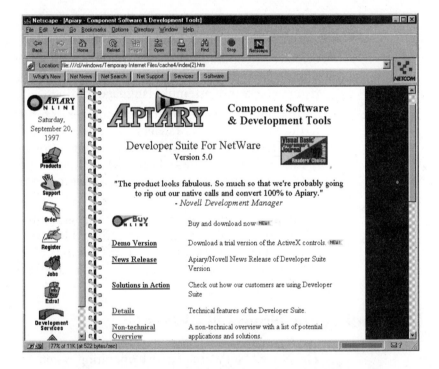

In this section, I will describe how to use the NetWare interrupt functions from within Visual Basic. Although I have no intention of covering all of the interrupt routines—these fill a couple of large reference books on their own—I have included a range of code examples that cover the common functions that you might encounter.

Declaring the NetWare interrupt calls

Novell NetWare functions are, by default, called using a range of DOS interrupts. Luckily, these have been wrapped in a DLL supplied by Novell—the NWCALLS.DLL library. Unfortunately, although this DLL covers all the NetWare functions, it does not have a convenient wrapper for Visual Basic. If you want to use any of the NetWare functions via this DLL you will first have to include function declarations in your VB project.

In the section below, I have included the declarations for a number of the NetWare functions that I will use later in this chapter. (These function declarations were provided from the research and work done by Steve Jackson and uploaded to CompuServe.)

```
Declare Function NWCallsInit Lib "nwcalls.dll" (ByVal lpArg1 As
Any, ByVal lpArg2 As Any) As Integer

Declare Function NWGetDriveStatus Lib "nwcalls.dll" (ByVal
driveNumber As Integer, ByVal pathFormat As Integer, status As
Integer, conn As Integer, ByVal rootPath As String, ByVal
relativepath As String, ByVal fullpath As String) As Integer

Declare Function NWGetConnectionList Lib "nwcalls.dll" (ByVal
mode As Integer, iConnectionList As Integer, ByVal connListSize
As Integer, numConnections As Integer) As Integer

Declare Function NWGetConnectionStatus Lib "nwcalls.dll" (ByVal
conn As Integer, conninfo As NW_CONN_INFO, ByVal structsize As
Integer) As Integer

Declare Function NWGetConnectionHandle Lib "nwcalls.dll" (ByVal
sServerName As String, ByVal mode As Integer, connHandle As
Integer, ByVal connScope As Any) As Integer

Declare Function NWGetPrimaryConnectionID Lib "nwcalls.dll"
(connHandle As Integer) As Integer

Declare Function NWAttachToFileServer Lib "nwcalls.dll" (ByVal
sServerName As String, ByVal scopeFlag As Integer, conn As
Integer) As Integer

Declare Function NWDetachFromFileServer Lib "nwcalls.dll"
(ByVal conn As Integer) As Integer

Declare Function NWLoginToFileServer Lib "nwcalls.dll" (ByVal
conn As Integer, ByVal sObjectName As String, ByVal objecttype
As Integer, ByVal sPassword As String) As Integer
```

```
Declare Function NWLogoutFromFileServer Lib "nwcalls.dll"
(ByVal conn As Integer) As Integer

Declare Function NWSetDriveBase Lib "nwcalls.dll" (ByVal
driveNumber As Integer, ByVal connHandle As Integer, ByVal
DirHandle As Integer, ByVal dirpath As String, ByVal driveScope
As Integer) As Integer

Declare Function NWDeleteDriveBase Lib "nwcalls.dll" (ByVal
driveNumber As Integer, ByVal nwscope As Integer) As Integer

Declare Function NWParseNetwarePath Lib "nwcalls.dll" (ByVal
filepath As String, conn As Integer, DirHandle As Integer, ByVal
newfilepath As String) As Integer
```

The NWGetConnectionStatus() function returns the details about
the current connection within a structure, NW_CONN_INFO. This holds the
server name, client name and current session details.

Using the NetWare functions

With the above declarations added to the start of your VB project file
and the NWCALLS.DLL file installed on your PC, you can start to use the
commands to quiz the NetWare shell about the network environment.

Figure 4.2:
Function
definitions
to use the
NetWare
library DLL.

The first command allows you to log in to a NetWare server directly from within the application. Unlike the Windows environment that requests user login details when it starts ups, the NetWare user-based security only kicks into action when the user tries to log in to the central server.

To log in to the NetWare server we will use the NWAttachToFileServer() API call to make the connection to the NetWare server and then use the NWLoginToFileServer() API call to pass the username and password on to the server for validation. The first function, NWAttachToFileServer(), is supplied with the name of the server that we want to attach to and in return supplies an integer handle that identifies the session between the workstation and server. We can pass this handle on to the NWLoginToFileServer() function together with our user details.

```
Sub Netware_Login ()

    Dim retValue As Integer
    Dim intSessionHandle As Integer
    Dim strServerName As String
    Dim strUserID As String
    Dim strPassword As String
    Dim intPwdLen As Integer

    convert string values to uppercase for NetWare convention

    strServerName = UCase$("Office_1")
    strUserID = UCase$("Simon")
    strPassword = UCase$("Password")
    intPwdLen = Len$(strPassword)
    'create session by attaching to server
    retValue = NWAttachToFileServer(strServerName, 0,
            intSessionHandle)
    'now login to server

    retValue = NWLoginToFileServer(intSessionHandle, strUserID,
            intPwdLen, strPassword)

End Sub
```

The NWAttachToFileServer() supplies a handle (between 1 and 8) in the intSessionHandle variable and returns a status code according to Table 4.1.

All the other functions in these examples only return one useful code, which is equal to zero when the action has completed successfully.

Table 4.1: *Status codes*

Return Code	Status
0	success
F8h	already attached
F9h	no free slots on server
FAh	no more server slots
FCh	unkown server
FEh	bindery locked
FFh	no response

Our second sample utility, again using the API functions, lets you log off from the server. This time, we start by retrieving the connection handle for the session using the NWGetConnectionHandle() function, then pass this to the NWLogoutFromFileServer() function. Although we have now logged out, there is still a link to the server since we attached to it; we should finish by detaching from the server.

```
Sub Logoff_Server()

    Dim retValue As Integer
    Dim intSessionHandle As Integer
    Dim strServerName As String
    Dim strUser As String
    Dim strPassword As String
    Dim Mode As Integer

    'convert string values to uppercase for NetWare convention
    strServerName = UCase$("Office_1")

    Mode = 0
    'get a handle to the current session
    retValue = NWGetConnectionHandle(strServerName, Mode,
            intSessionHandle, ByVal 0&)

    'use the handle to log off from the server
    retValue = NWLogoutFromFileServer(intSessionHandle)

    'finally, detach from the server
    retValue = NWDetachFromFileServer(intSessionHandle)

End Sub
```

The last utility lists the server names to which the user's workstation has connections. This starts by finding the total number of connections, then executes a simple loop that retrieves an object block NWInfo that contains details of each connection. From this structure, you can pull out the name of the server for the link, which is then added to a listbox. This routine uses the NetWare detail structure, which has the following format (the declaration should be at the start of your application).

```
Type NWINFO_OBJ

    conn As Integer
    Flags As Integer
    SessionID As Integer
    ConnNum As Integer
    ServerAddr As String * 12
    ServerType As Integer
    ServerName As String * 48
    ClientType As Integer
    clientname As String * 48

End Type

Sub List_Links()

    Dim retValue As Integer
    Dim i As Integer
    Dim ServerName As String
    Dim NWInfo As Type NWInfo_Obj
    Dim NWInfo_Size As Integer
    NWInfo_Size = Len(NWInfo)
    Dim intNumConnections As Integer
    'call to find the total number of connections in place

    retValue = NWGetConnectionList(0, intConnectionList(0), 100,
            intNumConnections)

    For i = 0 To intNumConnections - 1

        'get the info object block for each connection on the list,
        'store the details in NWInfo
        retValue = NWGetConnectionStatus(intConnectionList(i),
                NWInfo, NWInfo_Size)
        'strip out the server name from the object block
        ServerName = Left$(NWInfo.ServerName, InStr(NWInfo.
                ServerName, Chr(0)) -1)
        lstServers.AddItem ServerName

    Next i

End Sub
```

Third-party NetWare components

Although the NetWare API is made considerably easier to manage thanks to the NWCALLS.DLL, it is still difficult to handle the hundreds of different commands that the NetWare shell and server can process. To help sort out this problem, there are several add-in controls from third-party developers that will package all the NetWare functions within an easy-to-use VBX, OCX/ActiveX control. One of the most popular is the Apiary NetWare component (www.apiary.com). These third-party controls are excellent if you want to minimize development time and reduce the learning curve, but it is not difficult to use the API commands, and the Novell Web site and CompuServe forums are packed with technical support for developers who want to use the methods I have outlined above.

NetBIOS

Although perhaps beginning to show its age, NetBIOS is still one of the most widely used network protocols and networking systems available. It was introduced in the early 1980s to work with the first IBM PC network adapter and was driven by the Microsoft MS-Net software; since then, all IBM and Microsoft LAN software have used the NetBIOS interface and protocol as a basic building block in creating the low-level functions for a network.

One of the huge benefits of NetBIOS is that regardless of the network operating system that you are using, you will almost certainly find that it can support NetBIOS; some (such as Windows) support it in a native mode, wheras others (such as NetWare) support it as an option. However, once you have the support, you can use the same set of commands from your applications to access the network functions, which means your NetBIOS-aware VB application can carry out the same functions on an Windows NT network, DEC Pathworks or IBM LAN.

In order to access the NetBIOS functions from within VB you need to use one of the Windows 95 or NT API calls that will pass on the data structure to the underlying network system. In older versions of Windows, the same task required a complicated system of DOS interrupts and assembly-language routines that put most developers off the entire idea. In the following pages, I will describe the basic functionality of NetBIOS and how the NetBIOS Windows API function can be used. However, with the improvements to Windows and VB, I now find that I can create most of my applications without this API and if I do need it, I often turn to a third-party NetBIOS control.

Using NetBIOS

NetBIOS provides a wide set of commands that allow a developer to work, at a low level, with the network to provide links between applications on the network. These can be broadcast links in which one computer broadcasts a message to others, or it can be a controlled circuit between two applications. These features are often used for signaling and data exchange between applications, but you might find it easier to use the Network DDE and Remote OLE objects that are part of VB (and explained in Chapter 9)

NetBIOS services

The NetBIOS protocol provides a range of services for applications; these can be split into four categories: name management, connection-oriented data transfer, connectionless-oriented data transfer, and general-purpose services.

Name management
Every network adapter has its own unique address that is defined by the adapter's manufacturer and allows the adapter to be identified on any size of network. A computer also has a logical name (with up to 16 characters) that actually maps to the unique address, but provides a more manageable way for an application to use the address. A computer can support up to 254 logical names per adapter card. The advantage of using logical names is that it means an application can send data from one computer to another using the logical names and is not tied to the physical address defined in the adapter (which would wreck the program if you changed the adapter or moved the computer!).

To help manage these logical names, there are groups that can have many different names associated with this element (in contrast, there can only be one of each logical name in a LAN).

Connection-oriented data transfer
To allow two applications to create a virtual link between themselves within a network, NetBIOS provides a connection-oriented system called a *session*. A session can be established and then either computer can transfer data to the other computer in the session in a reliable way.

Connectionless-oriented data transfer
For situations where a private virtual link between two applications is not necessary, NetBIOS provides a connectionless-oriented link called a *datagram*. This allows one application to send data to one or more other applications with no guarantee of delivery. For example, if user ADMIN wants to send a message to the ten users, he can create ten ses-

sions and send the message or can send one datagram to all the users. Datagrams can be sent to a name, a group name, or as a broadcast message.

General-purpose services

To help manage the general business of a network application, NetBIOS includes a set of commands that provide network adapter status and help find a logical name on the network.

Controlling NetBIOS with the Network Control Block

The way in which you can send commands to NetBIOS and receive information back in return is by using a standard structure called a Network Control Block (NCB).

The NCB structure

```
typedef struct NCB {

    BYTE  ncb_command;
    BYTE  ncb_retcode;
    BYTE  ncb_lsn;
    BYTE  ncb_num;
    DWORD ncb_buffer;
    WORD  ncb_length;
    BYTE  ncb_callName[16];
    BYTE  ncb_name[16];
    BYTE  ncb_rto;
    BYTE  ncb_sto;
    DWORD ncb_post;
    BYTE  ncb_lana_num;
    BYTE  ncb_cmd_cplt;
    BYTE  ncb_reserved[14];

} NCB;
```

If you want to submit a command to NetBIOS, you use the ncb_command field in the NCB; on completion, the ncb_retcode field holds the return value, with 00h for success. Data for the command is stored in ncb_buffer, and the logical name of the remote computer is in ncb_callname.

The call itself takes just one argument: a pointer to the ncb block— Netbios(ncb).

NetBIOS commands

The range of commands available within NetBIOS is actually the range of codes that are supported within the ncb_command field of the NCB structure.

Table 4.2: *NetBIOS commands*

Code	Meaning
NCBACTION	provides extensions to the transport interface
NCBADDGRNAME	adds a group name to the local name table
NCBADDNAME	adds a unique name to the local name table
NCBASTAT	retrieves the status of the adapter. When this code is specified, the ncb_buffer member points to a buffer to be filled with an ADAPTER_STATUS structure, followed by an array of NAME_BUFFER structures
NCBCALL	opens a session with another logical or group name
NCBCANCEL	cancels a previous command
NCBCHAINSEND	sends the contents of two data buffers to the specified session partner
NCBCHAINSENDNA	sends the contents of two data buffers to the specified session partner and does not wait for acknowledgment
NCBDELNAME	deletes a name from the local name table
NCBDGRECV	receives a datagram from any name
NCBDGRECVBC	receives broadcast datagram from any host
NCBDGSEND	sends datagram to a specified name
NCBDGSENDBC	sends a broadcast datagram to every host on the LAN
NCBENUM	enumerates LAN adapter numbers for multiple adapters fitted in one PC. When this code is specified, the ncb_buffer member points to a buffer to be filled with a LANA_ENUM structure
NCBFINDNAME	determines the location of a name on the network. When this code is specified, the ncb_buffer member points to a buffer to be filled with a FIND_NAME_ HEADER structure followed by one or more FIND_NAME_BUFFER structures
NCBHANGUP	closes a specified session
NCBLANSTALERT	notifies the user of LAN failures that last for more than one minute
NCBLISTEN	enables a session to be opened with another name
NCBRECV	receives data from the specified session partner

Table 4.2: *NetBIOS commands (continued)*

Code	Meaning
NCBRECVANY	receives data from any session corresponding to a specified name
NCBRESET	resets a LAN adapter
NCBSEND	sends data to the specified computer within a session
NCBSENDNA	sends data to specified computer within a session but does not wait for an acknowledgment
NCBSSTAT	retrieves the status of the session. Returns information in the ncb_buffer element within a SESSION_HEADER structure
NCBTRACE	allows NCB tracing
NCBUNLINK	unlinks the adapter

NetBIOS return codes

Once the operation has been executed by NetBIOS, the ncb_retcode field contains the return code for the action. If it is equal to NRC_GOODRET, then the operation was succesful; any other return code indicates a problem.

Third-party NetBIOS controls

To add NetBIOS functionality to your VB application, you need to have a very good grasp of the NetBIOS interrupt and its NCB structure; because Visual Basic is designed for rapid development, most developers (myself included) will prefer to use one of the third-party VBX/OCX controls that provide NetBIOS commands within a neatly wrapped and familiar component.

Figure 4.3:
NetBIOS access components supplied by Apiary.

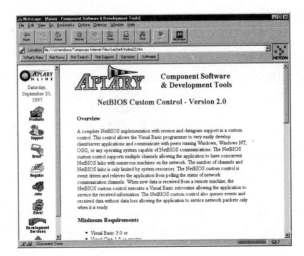

Again, Apiary (www.apiary.com) produces a good control that supports all the NetBIOS functions and is far easier to work with than the combination of Windows API calls and NetBIOS functions described above.

Conclusion

Both NetWare and NetBIOS offer a powerful set of network commands. The NetWare function set is very comprehensive, whereas the brief set of NetBIOS commands works at a very low level. In order to use the NetWare features you will need to download the support DLL provided by Novell and then use the simple function set. In comparison, NetBIOS is driven from a single Windows API call and is not for the fainthearted. In all honesty, I would tackle the NetWare functions as described, but for the NetBIOS routines I would either try to use the techniques covered in Chapter 9 or install a third-party NetBIOS support component.

5

Electronic Mail with MAPI

Introduction

There are two types of electronic mail that you might want to deal with: internal LAN mail and messages destined for users on the Internet. There are several different email standards that define how messages are transferred between the sender and receiver. The mail standards used for LAN-based messaging and for Internet or WAN-based messaging tend to fall into separate camps; sure, you can use a standard, such as X.500 for LAN-based networks, but it is rare and only useful if your local network has many different servers and hundreds of users. To tackle the problems of email, I have split the subject into two separate sections for the two main standards: in this chapter I cover the MAPI standard used to send mail over local area networks, and in Chapter 6 I cover the SMTP/POP3 standard used for Internet, mainframe, or other TCP/IP-based networks.

Email over local area networks

There are several standards that are widely supported as ways of transferring mail around a local area network. There is Microsoft's own standard, called MAPI (mail-API), which is supported by almost all of its applications. It is a good choice for Visual Basic mail applications because VB includes a component that does much of the hard work! Alternatives to MAPI include VIM (a rival standard supported by Lotus and other vendors) and MHS (an independent standard often used as a post office or gateway between different mail systems).

Using VB to create a simple electronic mail program means that you can create a product that is as simple or complex as you require. If you are developing for end users who have never used email, you can design the simplest mail program in just a few steps. To start with, you need not worry yourself or the user with attachments, type of delivery or receipts. Once the users have got into the swing of email, simply extend your mail program to add in the other functions—all are supported by the MAPI component and accessed by its properties or functions. A typical example would be to create a simple Windows mail application to access a text-only mainframe mail utility—once you have configured MAPI to deal with the mainframe's mail protocol, the front end is very simple to create.

Figure 5.1:
Microsoft Exchange uses MAPI calls to transfer email.

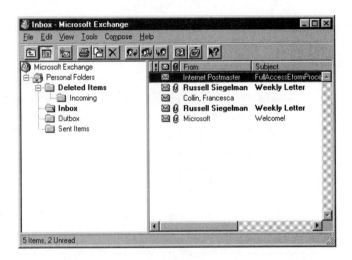

One of the most useful network applications is electronic mail. Windows 95 includes Microsoft Exchange, a fully featured email application that provides more than a simple messaging service. It can collect all your mail messages from different sources: from your local network, faxes, from CompuServe and even from the Internet. This chapter shows you how to configure, use, and get the best from Exchange using VB.

Windows mail client: Exchange

All of the MAPI controls direct commands from the VB application to the mail client installed on the user's computer. For Windows 3.11, this is the MS-Mail client and under Windows 95 the software is the Microsoft Exchange application. Exchange is a far more sophisticated version of the MS-Mail client that was included in Windows for Workgroups: it provides a single, central view of all your messages from different sources, including LAN, Internet, CompuServe and fax. Because MS-Mail and Exchange are driven by MAPI commands, you can develop a VB application that provides all the features of Exchange but from your own VB front end! If you have configured Exchange to support Internet mail or fax support, your VB MAPI-enabled application can also support these messaging systems.

The Exchange application that's included as part of Windows 95 is the client section—there's an Exchange server product that you can buy separately. However, you can build an email service for your workgroup within the network using just the client software supplied.

Exchange, like all Microsoft messaging applications, uses the MAPI standard to exchange messages between systems. This means that it can send and receive mail with any Microsoft Mail client or server or any other third-party MAPI-compliant product. It can also use bolt-on drivers that let it exchange messages with other non-MAPI services—supplied with Windows are drivers for CompuServe, Microsoft Network, and Microsoft Fax. If you want to exchange messages with any other software, such as Lotus cc:Mail (which is based on the VIM messaging API specification), then you will need to buy an additional gateway either to convert messages to a format Exchange can understand or from Exchange to the foreign format.

How Exchange works

Exchange is based on the concept of a central postoffice. If you want to use Exchange on your network, you will need to create a postoffice for the workgroup; if you have several workgroups on your network, each can have its own postoffice, but they cannot exchange messages unless you upgrade to Microsoft Mail or Exchange Server. The postoffice is actually just a folder structure that's stored on one designated computer—there are folders for each user and the messages to and from each user are stored here. The Exchange software on each workstation is used to check the user's folder for new messages and to save a message file into a user's folder when sending mail. Obviously, the postoffice folder structure should be located on a PC that's always switched on and that has enough disk capacity for the build-up of the message database. Lastly, the postoffice folder structure should be accessible to any authorized user on the network, and so needs to be set up as a shareable resource.

The Exchange postoffice

The folder structure that forms the postoffice needs to be created, named and located on a workstation using the Microsoft Mail Postoffice icon (in Control Panel) before you configure Exchange on any workstations. The version of the postoffice included with Windows is the workgroup edition and is similar, but not as flexible, as the Microsoft Mail Server or Exchange Server products that are available separately. The main limits to the workgroup edition are that it cannot exchange mail with users of other postoffices, there is no access to Microsoft Mail gateways, and the administrative tools are a simplified set of those found in the Server edition.

Figure 5.2:
The Exchange Address Book that can be accessed from VB.

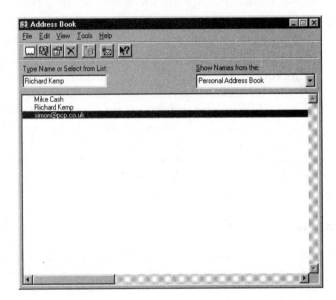

The Exchange client

This application uses MAPI calls to allow you to send and receive messages with any compliant service. In practice, this will normally mean any other Exchange user registered within the workgroup postoffice. However, you can extend the range of connectivity options by using MAPI service providers; these are extensions to the Exchange client that allow it to send and receive messages through a CompuServe account, via the Microsoft Network, the Internet, or via fax. Lastly, if you upgrade to the Server edition of the postoffice, your users can benefit from connectivity with other postoffices through LAN or WAN links controlled by the postoffice.

From the user's point of view, the Exchange client is accessed from the Desktop with the "InBox" icon. Double-click on this icon and it will start the application and check for any new mail in the postoffice and, if installed, on any MAPI service provider (such as Microsoft Network).

The Exchange front-end is based on folders that can be used to sort and organize your messages. These folders are arranged under each user's Personal Folder—which is actually another MAPI service provider—and is where all incoming and outgoing messages from any service providers are stored. Secondly, Exchange will support address books for each user (the Personal Address Book) or a public book (the Postoffice Address Book) or for an external service (such as for Microsoft Network). Again, the Address Book function is actually a MAPI service provider that extends the power of Exchange.

Figure 5.3:
Selecting the address book to use.

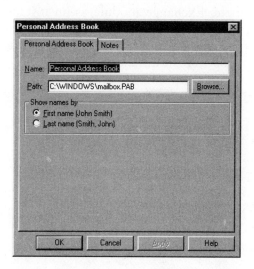

The two MAPI service providers we've mentioned are the unlikely candidates: Folder and Address Book. The main providers are used to link Exchange with other mail services. The main module is the Microsoft Mail Services MAPI service provider. This connects an Exchange client to either the workgroup or Server postoffice. In addition, Windows comes with the Microsoft Fax MAPI service provider, which lets you use Exchange to send or receive messages via a fax card. Recipients can be entered in any of the Address Books, and messages created using the familiar Exchange front-end. The CompuServe Mail MAPI service provider is also included with Windows and allows you to send and receive mail via a CompuServe account (which you will need to set up separately). Lastly, there is an Internet Mail MAPI service provider module, which forms part of the separate Windows 95 Plus! pack and allows users to exchange messages with any SMTP and POP3 service using the TCP/IP protocol.

Installing Windows Mail client support

A number of the Windows 95 components are optional during the install procedure. Some are installed by default; others can be installed either at this point or you can go back later and run the Add/Remove Programs utility from the Control Panel.

If you want to add connectivity options, fax, email, direct cable connections between a desktop and laptop and other similar options, then it's worth looking through the list rather than accepting the default. If you selected the Exchange module as an installed option, then the Setup program will automatically add an Inbox icon to your Desktop when it starts Windows and will run the Inbox Setup Wizard when you finish the main Windows installation.

Figure 5.4:
Exchange allows messages to be filtered to folders.

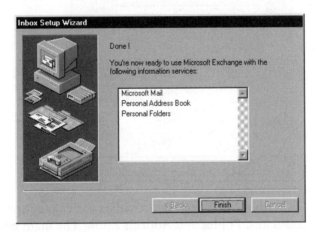

If you have already created a postoffice and added users to it, all this information will appear in the Inbox Setup Wizard and you can, effectively, skip through the process of creating a new Inbox very quickly.

Using the MAPI mail component

Visual Basic includes the MAPI mail component that allows developers to create mail front-end applications very easily. The VB program is not used for mail delivery, simply to access the mail messages in the user's InBox; the InBox and the mail delivery system is part of the Windows 95 Exchange client software or the Windows 3.x Mail client. This type of application is called a mail-enabled program and uses hooks to ask the MAPI services, provided as low-level routines in the system DLLs, to actually carry out the functions.

The delivery of mail between users is controlled by the mail postoffice. If you have a simple, single-server installation with each user running Windows 95 or 3.11, then you can use the Exchange/Mail client software to manage the simple postoffice. In this case, the postoffice is simply a shared directory structure with a subdirectory for each user. As a user logs in, the client software checks to see if there is any new mail (files) in the user's postoffice directory.

In a more complex, multi-server installation you will need to upgrade to a dedicated postoffice program. The simple client software supplied with Windows will not support multiple servers; instead you need to buy and install either Microsoft Mail Server or Microsoft Exchange Server. Both of these applications run as a dedicated program on a PC and actively manage mail messages, sending alerts to users as new mail arrives. The mail client and MAPI components can be used to access either of the above systems, if the postoffice can accept foreign mail via a gateway (available with the dedicated server postoffice) then the MAPI component can access these message.

NOTE

If you want to use the MAPI component, you must make sure that the user's PC has the MAPI DLLs installed, together with the basic mail client software—if not, you should install these options from the Windows 95 source CD.

The VB MAPI components are supplied as a VBX, OCX or ActiveX component depending upon the version of VB that you are using. Each works in a very similar way and there are no features that differ between them, so the examples in this chapter can be used on any platform.

Figure 5.5:
Adding MAPI controls to the form to complete the email application.

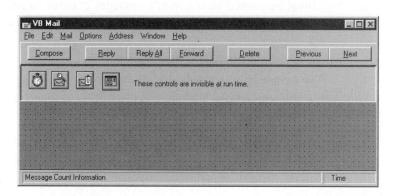

The MAPI controls

There are two main MAPI controls that give your VB applications access to the mail services of Microsoft Mail/Exchange installed in Windows. These two controls are MAPISession and MAPIMessages. The first, MAPISession, is used to establish a session, log on and log off; the second, MAPIMessages, is used to actually send, read and manipulate the messages.

With the MAPI controls, you can carry out a range of mail functions and can link in to the resources provided by the mail system client, including the following functions:

- access messages in the InBox
- compose a new message
- manage recipients of a message
- manage attachments of a message
- send messages
- manage messages (copy, delete)
- access the Address Book
- reply to or forward new incoming mail

MAPISession control

This control allows you to create a new session, sign on, sign off and ensure that the username and passwords are correct. Once you have placed the MAPISession icon on your form, it is invisible at run time and is controlled entirely via its properties and methods. This property must be used to establish a session before any messages can be sent or received; the MAPISession control will provide a SessionID handle that must be passed to the MAPIMessages control to carry out any message functions. The main properties for the MAPISession control are:

- Action
- DownloadMail
- LogonUI
- NewSession
- Password
- SessionID
- UserName

Action

Control	MAPISession property
Syntax	`object.Action = value`

Arguments		
	`value = 1`	logs the user into the account specified by the UserName and Password properties and returns a session handle in the SessionID property
	`value = 2`	ends the session and logs the user off the account

Use	defines the action that should occur when the MAPISession control is invoked. This property is only included for compatibility with older controls—try to use the newer properties instead. The Action property is only available as a write-only property at run time.

DownloadMail

Control	MAPISession property
Syntax	`object.DownloadMail = value`

Arguments		
	`value = True`	(default setting) all new messages on the mail server are transferred to the user's InBox during the login process
	`value = False`	new messages are not transferred during the login process. This speeds up login, but you will have to use another command to retrieve the messages at a later time

Use	defines how new mail is transferred during the login process

LogonUI

Control	MAPISession property
Syntax	`object.LogonUI = value`

Arguments		
	`value = True`	(default setting) dialog box is displayed for new users to prompt for their user name and password
	`value = False`	a dialog box is not displayed

Use	if the user does not have a username and password stored by the MAPI system, you should use the True argument to display a dialog

box, unless you have already stored their username and password using your own input screen.

NewSession

Control	MAPISession property
Syntax	`object.NewSession = value`
Arguments	`value = True` new session is started even if an existing session is open
	`value = False` (default) the existing session is used when a new session is requested
Use	to prevent too many sessions being started in error, when only one is required

Password

Control	MAPISession property
Syntax	`object.Password = value`
Arguments:	`value = string` contains the password for the user's account

SessionID

Control	MAPISession property
Syntax	`object.SessionID`
Use	returns the session handle for the current messaging session; only available at run time and used to get the handle to pass to the MAPIMessages control

SignOff

Control	MAPISession method
Syntax	`object.SignOff`
Use	ends the messaging session and signs the user off from the account (defined by the UserName property)

SignOn

Control	MAPISession method
Syntax	`object.SignOn`

Use	starts a messaging session and logs the user in to the account (defined by the UserName method)

UserName

Control	MAPISession property
Syntax	`object.UserName = value`
Arguments	`value = string` contains a string with the user's name
Use	defines the user's name that matches the password property and is used to sign in to an account

MAPIMessages control

This control allows you to manage the general message functions of a MAPI session, including creating new messages, sending and reading mail, adding attachments and managing the InBox. Once you have placed the MAPIMessages icon on your form, it is invisible at run time and is controlled entirely via its properties and methods. Before you can use this control, you must first establish a session using the MAPISession control. The MAPISession control provides a SessionID handle that must then be passed to the MAPIMessages control to carry out any message functions. The main properties for the MAPIMessages control are listed below.

Message buffers

When you are using the MAPIMessages control in your applications, you must ensure that your program can track two different message buffers: *compose buffer* and the *read buffer*.

Read buffer

Contains an indexed set of messages that have been retrieved from the InBox. The MsgIndex property is used to access an individual message from this buffer (starting at zero). The messages stored in this buffer are retrieved using the Fetch method and are filtered during this operation according to the FetchMsgType property and then sorted within the buffer according to the FetchSorted property. You can also use the FetchUnreadOnly property to define the type of message that is stored in this buffer. Note that any message stored in this buffer can be read, but cannot be written to or altered. If you want to allow a user to edit a message, then you have to copy the message to the compose buffer, which does allow editing.

Compose buffer
Contains any message that is being edited or has just been created. The compose buffers is used as the main working store for new messages and many of the functions will only work with this buffer. For example, you can only send a message from the compose buffers; you cannot send from the read buffer. To switch to the compose buffer, set the MsgIndex property of the control to –1 (any other value refers to a message in the read buffer).

Action

Control	MAPIMessages property
Syntax	`object.Action = value`

	Arguments		
		`MESSAGE_FETCH`	Fetch method
		`MESSAGE_SENDDLG`	Send method
		`MESSAGE_SEND`	Send method
		`MESSAGE_SAVEMSG`	Save method
		`MESSAGE_COPY`	Copy method
		`MESSAGE_COMPOSE`	Compose method
		`MESSAGE_REPLY`	Reply method
		`MESSAGE_REPLYALL`	ReplyAll method
		`MESSAGE_FORWARD`	Forward method
		`MESSAGE_DELETE`	Delete method
		`MESSAGE_SHOWADBOOK`	Show method
		`MESSAGE_SHOWDETAILS`	Show method
		`MESSAGE_RESOLVENAME`	ResolveName method
		`RECIPIENT_DELETE`	Delete method
		`ATTACHMENT_FETCH`	Fetch method

Use	this property is provided for backwards compatibility with VB 3; you should try to use the corresponding methods listed above rather than the value settings linked to this property.

AddressCaption

Control	MAPIMessages property
Syntax	`object.AddressCaption = value`
Arguments	`value = string` string value that defines the caption displayed at the top of the address book dialog box
Use	defines the caption that appears at the top of the address book dialog box when the Show method is used and its value is set to `False` (or is not specified)

AddressEditFieldCount

Control	MAPIMessages property
Syntax	`object.AddressEditFieldCount = value`

Arguments		
	`value = 0`	no edit controls are displayed; only allows browsing
	`value = 1`	(default) the To: edit control is displayed
	`value = 2`	the To: and CC: edit controls are displayed
	`value = 3`	the To:, CC: and BCC: edit controls are displayed
	`value = 4`	only the edit controls supported by the messaging transport system selected will be displayed (for example, BCC: will not be displayed for a fax message)

Use	defines the set of edit controls that are displayed within the address book dialog box when the Show method is used and its value is set to False (or is not specified)

AddressLabel

Control	MAPIMessages property
Syntax	`object.AddressLabel = value`

Arguments:		
	`value = string`	string value that defines the caption displayed for the To: field in the address book dialog box

Use	normally, this property is ignored, but if you do set it, it will change the caption label for the To: field in the address book dialog box.

AddressModifiable

Control	MAPIMessages property
Syntax	`object.AddressModifiable = value`

Arguments		
	`value = True`	user can modify his personal address book
	`value = False`	user cannot modify his personal address book

Use	defines whether a user can modify his personal address book

AddressResolveUI

Control	MAPIMessages property

Syntax	object.AddressResolveUI = value	
Arguments	value = True	dialog box is displayed with similar names that match the intended recipient's name, allowing the user to pick the correct, intended recipient
	value = False	dialog box is not displayed
Use	defines whether a dialog box is displayed in case of an ambiguous name in one of the message address fields found during the Resolve-Name method	

AttachmentCount

Control	MAPIMessages property
Syntax	object.AttachmentCount
Use	returns the number of attachments linked to the current message; only available at run time

AttachmentIndex

Control	MAPIMessages property	
Syntax	object.AttachmentIndex = value	
Arguments	value = long	long value that specifies the attachment to select from the current message
Use	used to define the particular attachment from a list of attachments linked to a message. The range of numbers for this property lies between 0 and AttachmentCount-1. As the different attachments linked to a message are referenced using this property, so the values of the other attachment properties change to reflect the attachment you are currently pointing at (AttachmentName, Attachment-PathName, AttachmentPosition, AttachmentType).	

If you want to add or delete an attachment, you should use the AttachmentCount and Delete properties respectively, but first remember to switch to the compose buffer by setting the MsgIndex property to –1.

AttachmentName

Control	MAPIMessages property
Syntax	object.AttachmentName

Use	returns a string that contains the name of the file or OLE object class type of the currently indexed attachment

AttachmentPathName

Control	MAPIMessages property
Syntax	`object.AttachmentPathName = value`
Arguments	`value = string` — string value that defines the full path name of the attachment file (only available if the MsgIndex property is set to –1). Otherwise is a read-only property that returns the full path of the currently indexed attachment
Use	used to define or retrieve the full path of the currently indexed attachment

AttachmentPosition

Control	MAPIMessages property
Syntax	`object.AttachmentPosition = value`
Arguments	`value = long` — long value that defines the position within the message body text of the attachment if the MsgIndex property is set to –1 or returns the position within the message body text
Use	used to define or retrieve the position (in relative character terms) of the currently indexed attachment within the message body text. For example, if the message is 20 characters long, you can place the attachment anywhere between 0 and 19.

AttachmentType

Control	MAPIMessages property
Syntax	`object.AttachmentType = value`
Arguments	`value = 0 = mapData` — attachment is a data file
	`value = 1 = mapEOLE` — attachment is an embedded OLE object
	`value = 2 = mapSOLE` — attachment is a static OLE object
Use	used to define or retrieve the type of data stored as an attachment. If you want to define the type, then the MsgIndex property must be set to –1; otherwise this property will return the type of the currently indexed attachement.

Compose

Control	MAPIMessages method
Syntax	`object.Compose`
Use	clears all the properties of the compose buffer and sets the MsgIndex to –1; used to switch to the mode that allows a user to create a message.

Copy

Control	MAPIMessages method
Syntax	`object.Copy`
Use	copies the currently indexed message into the compose buffer and switches to this buffer; sets the MsgIndex property to –1

Delete

Control	MAPIMessages method
Syntax	`object.Delete value`
Arguments	`value = 0 = mapMessageDelete` deletes all the parts of the currently indexed message, reduces MsgCount by one
	`value = 1 = mapRecipientDelete` deletes the currently indexed recipient and reduces the RecipCount property by one
	`value = 2 = mapAttachmentDelete` deletes the currently indexed attachment and reduces the AttachmentCount property by one
Use	deletes a message, recipient or attachment

Fetch

Control	MAPIMessages method
Syntax	`object.Fetch`
Use	creates a list of messages from the messages that have been selected from the InBox. The messages stored in the read buffer are retrieved using the Fetch method and are filtered during this operation according to the FetchMsgType property and then sorted within the buffer according to the FetchSorted property. You can also use the

FetchUnreadOnly property to define the type of message that is stored in this buffer.

Note that any message stored in this buffer can be read, but cannot be written to or altered. If you want to allow a user to edit a message, then you have to copy the message to the compose buffer, which does allow editing.

FetchMsgType

Control	MAPIMessages property
Syntax	`object.FetchMsgType = value`
Arguments	`value = string` string value that is used to filter and select the type of message retrieved from the InBox during the Fetch method. This value is dependent upon the type of message supported by the messaging system—unless you are sure of the type of message, leave this null to select the default message type
Use	specifies the type of message to select during a Fetch method

FetchSorted

Control	MAPIMessages property
Syntax	`object.FetchSorted = value`
Arguments	`value = True` messages are added to the read buffer list in the order they were received
	`value = False` (default) messages are added to the read buffer list in the order specified by the user's InBox
Use	creates a list of messages from the messages that have been selected from the InBox

FetchUnreadOnly

Control	MAPIMessages property
Syntax	`object.FetchUnreadOnly = value`
Arguments	`value = True` (default) only unread messages (that match other selection criteria) are retrieved during the Fetch method

	`value = False` all messages (that match other selection criteria) are retrieved during the Fetch method
Use	creates a list of messages from the messages that have been selected from the InBox

Forward

Control	MAPIMessages method
Syntax	`object.Forward`
Use	copies the currently indexed message to the compose buffer as a forwarded message and adds the letters "FW:" at the beginning of the Subject line; also sets the MsgIndex property to –1

MsgConversationID

Control	MAPIMessages property
Syntax	`object.MsgConversationID = value`
Arguments	`value = string` string value that specifies the thread of the currently indexed message; this is normally a read-only value unless the MsgIndex property is –1
Use	used to view the conversation thread of a message; used to track a message and its replies or related messages

MsgCount

Control	MAPIMessages property
Syntax	`object.MsgCount`
Use	returns the total number of messages in the read buffer retrieved during the last Fetch operation

MsgDateReceived

Control	MAPIMessages property
Syntax	`object.MsgDateReceived`
Use	returns the date and time at which the currently indexed message was received; the time and date are returned in the following YYYY/MM/DD HH:MM format in which the HH hour setting is in the 24-hour time system.

MsgID

Control	MAPIMessages property
Syntax	`object.MsgID`
Use	returns the unique, message-specific string identifier for the currently indexed message. The ID is a 64-character string.

MsgIndex

Control	MAPIMessages property
Syntax	`object.MsgIndex = value`
Arguments	`value = long` specifies the index value of the current message; can be set to move to a new message or read to find the position in the read buffer index. The range of values lies between 0 to MsgCount-1
Use	specifies the index of the message in the read buffer; if the value is −1 this means that a new message is being edited in the compose buffer.

MsgNoteText

Control	MAPIMessages property
Syntax	`object.MsgNoteText = value`
Arguments	`value = string` string value that defines the message body text for the message
Use	contains the entire text of a message, with each paragraph separated by a carriage return-line feed pair (0x0d0a)

MsgOrigAddress

Control	MAPIMessages property
Syntax	`object.MsgOrigAddress`
Use	returns the address of the sender of currently indexed message; if you send a message, this value is set for you by the delivery system

MsgOrigDisplayName

Control	MAPIMessages property
Syntax	`object.MsgOrigDisplayName`

Use	returns the username of the sender of currently indexed message; if you send a message, this value is set for you by the delivery system

MsgRead

Control	MAPIMessages property
Syntax	`object.MsgRead`
Use	returns either `True` or `False` depending on whether the message has been read or is still unread; note that if you access the message body or attachment, the message is marked as read—if you read just the header information it is not marked as read

MsgReceiptRequested

Control	MAPIMessages property
Syntax	`object.MsgReceiptRequested = value`
Arguments	`value = True`	a notification message will be sent to the sender when the recipient opens the message
	`value = False`	(default) no notification is generated when the message is opened
Use	returns a receipt message to the sender when the recipient opens the message

MsgSent

Control	MAPIMessages property
Syntax	`object.MsgSent`
Use	specifies whether the currently indexed message has been sent to the main postoffice or mail server for distribution to the recipient

MsgSubject

Control	MAPIMessages property
Syntax	`object.MsgSubject = value`
Arguments	`value = string`	specifies or returns the subject line of a message; if the message is being composed (MsgIndex = −1), this property will define the subject line; otherwise this property returns the subject line of the currently indexed message

| Use | returns or sets the subject of the currently indexed message |

MsgType

Control	MAPIMessages property
Syntax	`object.MsgType = value`
Arguments	`value = string`	string that specifies or returns the type of the message; if the message is being composed (MsgIndex = −1), this property will define the type of the message, which is usually IPM for Microsoft mail
Use	returns or sets the type string field of the message, for LANs; usually ignored unless you know the types of message supported by your particular mail server or gateway

RecipAddress

Control	MAPIMessages property
Syntax	`object.RecipAddress = value`
Arguments	`value = string`	string that specifies or returns the recipient's address of the message; if the message is being composed (MsgIndex = −1), this property will set the recipient's address
Use	returns or sets the recipient's address field of the message

RecipCount

Control	MAPIMessages property
Syntax	`object.RecipCount`
Use	returns (as a long integer) the total number of recipients of the currently indexed message

RecipDisplayName

Control	MAPIMessages property
Syntax	`object.RecipDisplayName = value`
Arguments	`value = string`	string that specifies or returns the name (not the address) of the recipient of the message; if the message is being composed (MsgIndex = −1), this property will define the recipient's name for this message

| Use | returns or sets the name of the recipient, displayed in the message header |

RecipIndex

Control	MAPIMessages property
Syntax	`object.RecipIndex = value`
Arguments	`value = long`	index number used to set a recipient from the list of recipients of the message; to add a new recipient, set the RecipIndex property to one greater than the current total (equal to RecipCount-1)
Use	sets the particular recipient from the list of recipients of a message

RecipType

Control	MAPIMessages property
Syntax	`object.RecipType = value`
Arguments	`value = 0 = mapOrigList`	message originator
	`value = 1 = mapToList`	current recipient is main recipient
	`value = 2 = mapccList`	current recipient is copy recipient
	`value = 3 = mapBccList`	current recipient is blind copy recipient
Use	returns or specifies the type of the currently indexed recipient; will return the current type of recipient unless MsgIndex = –1, in which case it will set the type of the current recipient

Reply

Control	MAPIMessages method
Syntax	`object.Reply`
Use	replies to a message by copying current message to the compose buffer and adds the text "RE:" to the beginning of the Subject line and sets the MsgIndex to –1

ReplyAll

| Control | MAPIMessages method |
| Syntax | `object.ReplyAll` |

| Use | replies to all the recipients of a message by copying current message to the compose buffer and adds the text "RE:" to the beginning of the Subject line and sets the MsgIndex to –1 |

ResolveName

Control	MAPIMessages method
Syntax	`object.ResolveName`
Use	verifies and confirms (resolves) the correct name of the currently indexed recipient by searching the address book—see also Address-ResolveUI

Save

Control	MAPIMessages method
Syntax	`object.Save`
Use	saves the message that is currently being edited in the compose buffer

Send

Control	MAPIMessages method
Syntax	`object.Send = value`
Arguments	`value = True`	sends a message using a dialog box to prompt the user for various message information, such as the address, subject and so on
	`value = False`	sends the message to the server without the dialog box prompt; any missing information will generate an error from the message server
Use	sends a message to the delivery server or postoffice	

SessionID

Control	MAPIMessages method
Syntax	`object.SessionID = value`
Arguments	`value = long`	long value that contains the handle of the current session

Use	use the MAPISession control to define a session and generate a session handle to pass to this property

Show

Control	MAPIMessages method
Syntax	`object.Show value`
Arguments	`value = True` displays a dialog box with the details of the current recipient
	`value = False` (default) displays the address book dialog box that allows a user to change the recipient of the message
Use	displays the address book dialog box or a simple dialog box to allow the user to check recipient details

Writing a MAPI mail application

To create a MAPI mail application, first make sure that the MAPI system is installed on your computer (see earlier in this chapter) and that you have installed the MAPI controls within Visual Basic. Since the MAPI controls generate messages that control the Microsoft Mail or Exchange client (depending upon the version of Windows), you will often see dialog boxes from these clients displayed. In almost all cases, it is possible to suppress these dialog boxes by supplying the information required—you will see how each method looks to the user throughout the following examples.

The basic email program

Start by dragging the MAPISession and MAPIMessages control icons onto your main program form. Enter the following code:

```
Private Sub Form_Load()
   MAPISession1.SignOn
   MAPISession1.SignOff
End Sub
```

Figure 5.6:
*The code
required to
run a MAPI
application
can be very
basic.*

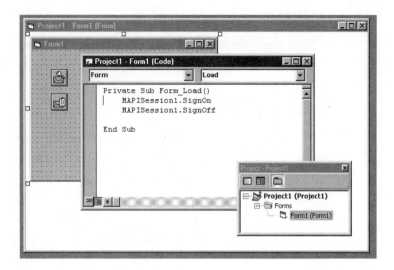

This displays the Exchange login screen prompting for the username and password before signing in the user to the mail server, then promptly signing off again. To get rid of this username prompt screen, simply provide the basic information that the MAPISession control requires so that the program code now looks like:

```
Private Sub Form_Load()

    'simple sign on without dialog box

    MAPISession1.UserName = "Simon"
    MAPISession1.Password = "password"
    MAPISession1.SignOn
    MAPISession1.SignOff

End Sub
```

Figure 5.7:
*Sign On to
choose a
profile within
Exchange.*

Using **MAPIMessages** control

Now that we have established a simple automatic login to the mail account for "Simon," let's use the MAPIMessages control to look at the messages in the InBox.

```
Private Sub Form_Load()

    'simple program to read the number of messages in the InBox
    MAPISession1.UserName = "Simon"
    MAPISession1.Password = "password"
    MAPISession1.SignOn
    MAPIMessages1.SessionID = MAPISession1.SessionID
    'assign SessionID

    MAPIMessages1.Fetch 'get all messages in InBox
                        'display number of messages

    MsgBox "Total Message: " + Str(MAPIMessages1.Msgcount)
    MAPISession1.SignOff

End Sub
```

Figure 5.8:
*Code required
to login and
collect email.*

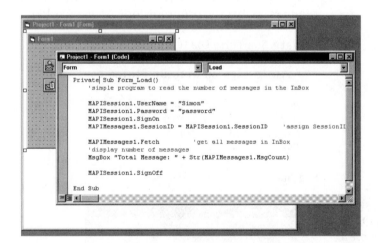

This program could be extended using a standard ListBox control to view the subject headers of each mail message that is waiting in the InBox. For this example, add a ListBox control to the form.

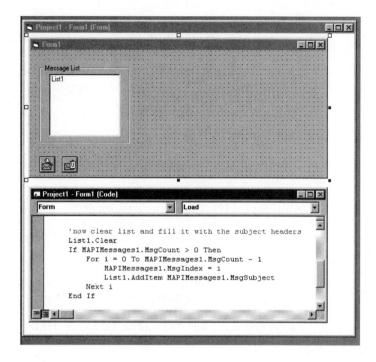

Figure 5.9:
Filling in a list box with the subject line from email.

```vb
Private Sub Form_Load()

    'simple program to read the number of messages in the InBox
    Dim i As Integer
    MAPISession1.UserName = "Simon"
    MAPISession1.Password = "password"
    MAPISession1.SignOn
    MAPIMessages1.SessionID = MAPISession1.SessionID
    'assign SessionID
    MAPIMessages1.Fetch              'get all messages in InBox
                                     'display number of messages
    MsgBox "Total Message: " + Str(MAPIMessages1.Msgcount)

    'now clear list and fill it with the subject headers
    List1.Clear

    if MAPIMessages1.MsgCount > 0 then
        for i = 0 to MAPIMessages1.MsgCount - 1
            MAPIMessages1.MsgIndex = i
            List1.AddItem MAPIMessages1.MsgSubject
        next i
    End If
    MAPISession1.SignOff

End Sub
```

At the other end of the process, you need to be able to send a message as well as access the number of messages in the InBox. Again, using the MAPIMessages control, we use the Compose and Send methods. You will notice that, because we have not supplied the header or message text information from within the program, the MAPI controls will display the default Exchange front-end.

```
Private Sub Form_Load()

    'simple program to send mail, with the Exchange dialog box

    MAPISession1.UserName = "Simon"
    MAPISession1.Password = "password"
    MAPISession1.SignOn
    MAPIMessages1.SessionID = MAPISession1.SessionID
    'assign SessionID

    MAPIMessages1.Compose
    'switch to compose mode, clear the buffer
    MAPIMessages1.Send True
    'send message, but using the Exchange dialog
    MAPISession1.SignOff

End Sub
```

The next part of this simple email program is to display the address book that allows the user to choose the recipient from the Exchange Address Book. Again, since the information supplied by the program does not provide enough detail, the MAPI system will display the default Exchange dialog box.

```
Private Sub Form_Load()

    'simple program to display the Exchange Address Book dialog box

    MAPISession1.UserName = "Simon"
    MAPISession1.Password = "password"
    MAPISession1.SignOn
    'assign SessionID
    MAPIMessages1.SessionID = MAPISession1.SessionID
    'show the address book
    MAPIMessages1.Show

    MAPISession1.SignOff

End Sub
```

Figure 5.10:
Accessing the Exchange Address Book within a MAPI session.

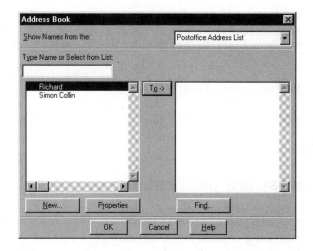

The final part of this simple email program is to allow attachments. This way, a user can send files and OLE objects via the mail system. The simplest way of allowing attachments is to leave the work to the Exchange dialog box, which already has a button for attachments, but this means that you would not really need to use the MAPI controls at all. In this example, we will define the attachment and message text from within the program, then display the Exchange dialog box to see the result before sending it.

```
Private Sub Form_Load()

    'simple program to define an attachment from within the program

    MAPISession1.UserName = "Simon"
    MAPISession1.Password = "password"
    MAPISession1.SignOn
    'assign SessionID
    MAPIMessages1.SessionID = MAPISession1.SessionID

    'switch to compose mode, clear the buffer
    MAPIMessages1.Compose
    MAPIMessages1.MsgSubject = "Our first attachment"

    'now our message text

    MAPIMessages1.MsgNoteTet = "Here is the project outline file" +
    Chr$(13)

    'now define the attachment at the start of the message

    MAPIMessages1.AttchmentPosition = 1
```

```
MAPIMessages1.AttachmentType = mapData
MAPIMessages1.AttachmentName = "Project X file"
MAPIMessages1.PathName = "C:\DOCS\PROJECT.DOC"

'send message, but using the Exchange dialog box
MAPIMessages1.Send True

MAPISession1.SignOff

End Sub
```

Creating a mail-aware application

It is unlikely that you will need to write a full email application from scratch on a regular basis, although it might be your first approach to making a mainframe mail system easier to use. The most common use for MAPI controls is to provide mail functions within other standard applications to produce a mail-aware application. If you have used any of the current Microsoft applications, such as Word, Excel, or Access, you will have seen the Send command in the File menu that allows you to send your current working document, spreadsheet or database as an email directly from within the application.

It is easy to provide this functionality for your VB applications by using the MAPI commands. For example, if you have a telephone order-taking application within VB, and your operators begin to get calls pointing out that the product is twice the price of a rival's gizmo, then you could add a Send command to allow the operator to send a comment to the supervisor.

The Send command would, in this case, only send mail to a pre-defined user—the supervisor—and would present a simple edit box for the operator's comment. In this way the Exchange dialog box would be hidden and the message interface would be kept as simple as possible.

The following two routines would work with your existing application and would log into the mail server and then display a simple form with an edit box and a couple of OK/Cancel buttons. Once the operator clicks on OK, the message is sent and the form cleared from view.

Figure 5.11:
The Send To menu command gives users access to email and messaging.

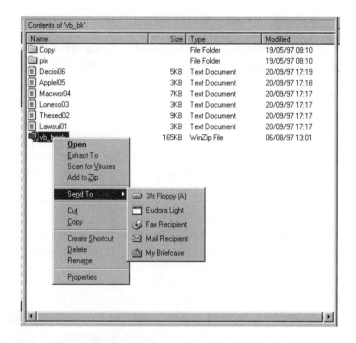

```
Private Sub SendMemo ()

    'first login as the operator

    MAPISession1.UserName = "Operator1"
    MAPISession1.Password = "password"
    MAPISession1.SignOn
    'assign SessionID
    MAPIMessages1.SessionID = MAPISession1.SessionID

    'now clear the edit box called Edit1

    Edit1.Clear

    'once the user has clicked on a button, log off

    MAPISession1.SignOff

End Sub
```

Now here is the code for the OK button on the form:

```
Private Sub Command1_Click(Index As Integer)

    MAPIMessages1.Compose
    'switch to compose mode, clear the buffer
```

```
MAPIMessages1.MsgSubject = "Memo from Operator1"
MAPIMessages1.MsgNoteText = Edit1
MAPIMessages1.RecipAddress = "supervisor"
'send message, without the Exchange dialog
MAPIMessages1.Send

End Sub
```

These are the basic steps required. Of course, you must add in error trapping—which I have omitted from all the examples for clarity—and you should add checks to make sure that the message text exists.

NOTE

If you do have an order or stock taking application, you could see how easy it would be to add in a routine that automatically sends an email in case stock levels of a product have run dangerously low; then no operator intervention would be required!

Figure 5.12: *A way of adding feedback to an application with a canned email line.*

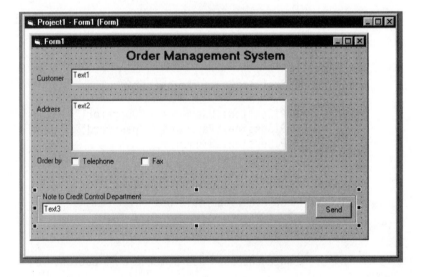

6

Email with SMTP/POP3

Introduction

In the previous chapter, I covered the methods of transferring messages over a network using the MAPI calls. This provides a useful way of integrating your VB applications with the mail client and server and makes it very easy to mail-enable any VB application. However, if you want to send mail over any TCP/IP network—in particular the Internet or an internal intranet—then you need to look to two new mail protocols to do the job. You could carry out the same functionality using MAPI, but you would need to rely on and reconfigure the Exchange client for internal TCP/IP mail and buy and install the Exchange Server software for external links.

In this chapter I cover the ways of sending and receiving messages over a TCP/IP network using the two popular protocols SMTP and POP3. I will be using the suite of Internet controls that was originally supplied by Microsoft as the well-known MS-ICP suite, but is now available from NetMasters. The suite is still called the Internet Control Pack, and provides a range of functions to allow a VB application to establish a TCP/IP session and transfer email using SMTP/POP3. These controls are bundled together as a 32-bit ActiveX control, which is great if you are using one of the newer versions of VB and running the applications under Windows 95 or NT. If you need to develop 16-bit applications, look to the VBX libraries available from Aviary and Crescent and see if these provide the functions that you require (these libraries are also available as OCX and ActiveX controls for 32-bit development).

For a general introduction to TCP/IP, read Chapter 8 on TCP/IP and socket programming.

Electronic mail: SMTP/POP3

Electronic mail over the Internet (or any TCP/IP-based network) normally uses a pair of protocols called SMTP (simple mail transport protocol) and POP3 (post office protocol). The way in which you use the protocols depends a lot on the type of mail server that is used by your ISP. However, almost all ISPs (with a few notable exceptions) use the following scheme:

Send mail from client to ISP's mail server	SMTP
Send mail between mail servers	SMTP
Read mail from ISP's mail server to client	POP3
Read mail between mail servers	SMTP

Figure 6.1:
Installing the suite of NetMasters components.

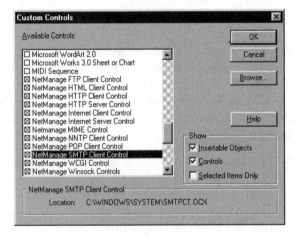

The SMTP mail protocol is the natural way of transferring mail over the Internet, but it normally requires each end to have a permanent link to the Internet; hence, it is used between servers. Some ISPs that offer an SMTP-only mail service (such as Demon Internet in the UK) have configured their version of SMTP to temporarily store the mail until the client dials in. Usually, SMTP mail servers do not store the mail and, if the receiver server is not available, the mail will be returned as undeliverable.

POP3 was developed to get around the lack of temporary message store in SMTP. It is usually only used by client software to contact the ISP's mail server to read new messages. If you look at any of the commercial email products, such as Eudora, Microsoft Internet Mail, or

Netscape Mail, you will be asked for the SMTP mail server to send mail and the POP3 mail server to receive mail.

As a quick conclusion, if you are writing your own mail server (see later in this chapter), you will need to fully understand SMTP send and receive; if you are using VB to create a client email application, you need to use SMTP to send and POP3 to receive. Both protocols are available as components within the NetMaster Internet Control Pack—simply drag the control onto your form.

Sending mail with SMTP

The SMTP protocol is really just a set of simple English-language type commands and responses that are exchanged between a client and a mail server. The client connects to the SMTP mail server using the TCP/IP port 25 (see Chapter 8 for more on TCP/IP ports); once connected to the mail server, the client identifies itself and asks if there is any new mail. New mail messages are sent as plain ASCII text—the end of a message is identified by a full stop by itself on a line. One point worth noting is that SMTP servers are not bothered about security—you need only supply the local client name!

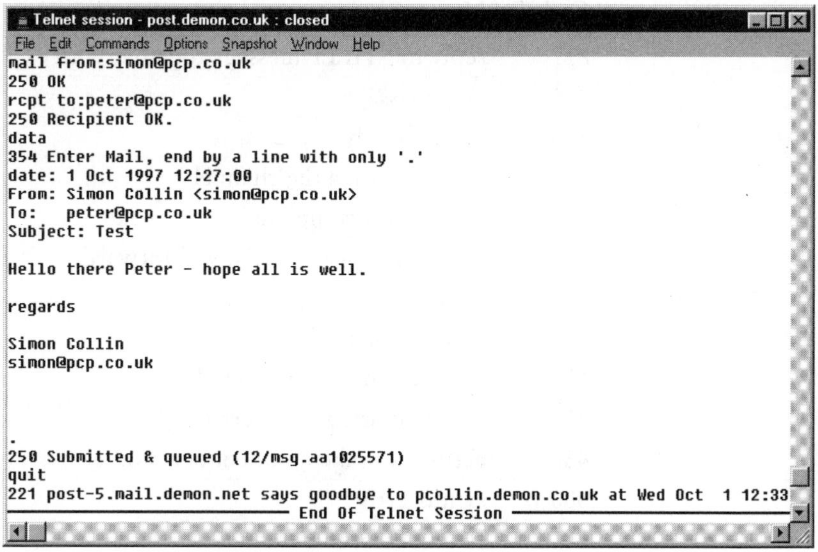

Figure 6.2:
A Telnet
conversation
with an SMTP
server show-
ing protocol to
send mail.

```
≡ Telnet session - post.demon.co.uk : closed                            _ □ ✕
 File  Edit  Commands  Options  Snapshot  Window  Help
mail from:simon@pcp.co.uk
250 OK
rcpt to:peter@pcp.co.uk
250 Recipient OK.
data
354 Enter Mail, end by a line with only '.'
date: 1 Oct 1997 12:27:00
From: Simon Collin <simon@pcp.co.uk>
To:   peter@pcp.co.uk
Subject: Test

Hello there Peter - hope all is well.

regards

Simon Collin
simon@pcp.co.uk



.
250 Submitted & queued (12/msg.aa1025571)
quit
221 post-5.mail.demon.net says goodbye to pcollin.demon.co.uk at Wed Oct  1 12:33
─────────────────── End Of Telnet Session ───────────────────
```

Table 6.1: *The SMTP commands*

Command	Meaning
DATA	main body of the email message
HELO <domain>	identifies the local client to the mail server
HELP <string>	provides information about the commands available on the server
MAIL FROM: <reverse path>	starts message transfer by supplying sender's mail address
QUIT	disconnects from the mail server
RCPT TO: <forward path>	mail address of recipient; multiple recipients should be supplied on separate lines

When the client issues one of the SMTP commands (above), the mail server responds with a three-digit response code that means that the command completed successfully or that there was an error.

Table 6.2: *SMTP server response commands*

Code	Meaning
211	reply to a HELP message together with explanatory text
214	help message
220	service ready
221	service closing the channel
250	mail action completed
251	specified user not local, will forward
354	start mail
421	service not available
450	mail action not completed
451	action aborted, local error
452	action not taken, not enough storage
500	syntax error
501	syntax error in parameters
502	command not implemented on server
503	bad sequence of commands
504	command parameter not implemented on server

Table 6.2: *SMTP server response commands (continued)*

Code	Meaning
550	action not taken
551	user not local
552	mail action aborted—exceeds server storage
553	action not taken
554	transaction failed

Figure 6.3:
*Configuring
the SMTP
component.*

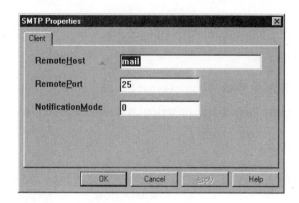

Using the SMTP control

NetMaster's ICP control includes an SMTP control that you can use to manage an SMTP session between the client and a remote mail server to send new mail. To use the control, drag the icon onto your main application form; the SMTP control is operated using a set of properties, methods and events, described below.

Figure 6.4:
*MIME
config dialog
defining an
attachment.*

Busy
property

`SMTPObject.Busy`

Returns `True` if the control is currently executing a command (and cannot accept a new command)

Cancel
method

`SMTPObject.Cancel`

Enters a request to cancel the current operation; once it has been cancelled, the Cancel event is triggered

DoInput
property

`SMTPObject.DocInput`

Returns a handle to the DocInput object that is used to send data to the control—there is no DocOutput object, since the POP3 control is used to send data

EnableTimer
property

`SMTPObject.EnableTimer(event) = bolValue`

Controls a timer for a particular event, where event can be one of three values and the `bolValue` is `True` if the timer is enabled and `False` if it is disabled:

`event = 1`	TimeOut is triggered if a connection is not made in time
`event = 2`	TimeOut is triggered if no data arrives in the period
`event = 65`	TimeOut is triggered according to a user-defined event

Errors
property

`SMTPObject.Errors`

Returns an error object (`icError`) that contains the last error

**Notification-
Mode**
property

`SMTPObject.NotificationMode = intValue`

Defines when notification is reported to the application where:

`intValue = 0`	notification is reported when the action has completed
`intValue = 1`	notification is reported when new data is received

**Protocol-
State**
property

`SMTPObject.ProtocolState`

Defines the state of the protocol being used by the control, returns one of the following three values:

integer returned	meaning
0	initial state, before a connection is established
1	authorization state, once a connection is open but before user authentication
2	transaction state, client has logged in and a full interactive link is available

RemoteHost
property

`SMTPObject.RemoteHost = strValue`

Property where `strValue` contains the URL or IP address of the remote host; use the Connect method to define and then make the connection

RemotePort
property

`SMTPObject.RemotePort = lngValue`

Property that defines the TCP/IP port being used for the SMTP control —normally port 25

ReplyCode
property

`SMTPObject.ReplyCode`

Returns a long integer reply value with the last reply code generated by the SMTP mail server

ReplyString
property

`SMTPObject.ReplyString`

Returns a string reply value with the last reply text generated by the SMTP mail server

SendDoc
method

`SMTPObject.SendDoc strURL, DocHeaders, varData, varFile, strOutput`

Used to transfer a file from the local computer to the remote mail server; the main argument is a DocInput object that is set up by the DocInput and URL properties

variable	meaning
strURL	string containing the name of the file on the remote host in the format "Mailto://remotehost/filename"
DocHeaders	header information as a DocHeaders object
varData	data buffer with any data to be transferred
varFile	file to be transferred
strOutput	string with the name of a file on the local machine where the reply document should be stored

State
property

`SMTPObject.State`

Returns an integer that defines the current state of the connection

integer returned	meaning
1	connecting, connection requested and waiting for acknowledgement
2	resolving host, waiting for translation of a URL to an IP address
3	host resolved, successful translation of a URL to an IP address
4	connected, connection has been established
5	disconnecting, request to disconnect
6	disconnected, no connection

TimeOut
property

`SMTPObject.TimeOut(event) = lngValue`

(Used with EnableTimer property) `lngValue` contains the length of the timer period used for the specified event

`event = 1`	TimeOut is triggered if a connection is not made in time
`event = 2`	TimeOut is triggered if no data arrives in the period
`event = 65`	TimeOut is triggered according to a user-defined event

URL
property

`SMTPObject.URL = strValue`

Contains the full name and path of the document being received or of a document requested by the DocInput property and retrieved with the SendDoc method

Programming with the SMTP control

The SMTP control makes it easy to send mail messages to a remote SMTP server, even if the number of properties might give the opposite impression! To create a new mail message is a simple three-step operation. In the first, we collect together the information required for the message, including the header details and the message itself. In the second step, we build a DocHeaders structure with this information, and in the third step we can actually fire the completed message off to the SMTP mail server.

```
From.text = POP3.UserID & "@" & POP3.RemoteHost
Date.text = Format(Date, "ddd, dd mmm yyyy ") & Format(Time,
"hh:mm:ss ")
```

These first two lines fill in the text fields of the two controls on the form that contain the From and Date/Time lines for the message. Normally, these fields would not be displayed since they should be internal to the system. I have provided extra text fields to allow the user to enter the subject, To, and message body text.

Figure 6.5:
A simple form implementing an email application.

Now, before sending the message we need to build up a DocHeaders structure so that it contains the information for the message header.

```
Dim dh As DocHeaders
```

Our first line defines the dh variable as an instance of the DocHeaders library structure. This will then be filled with the basic header information for this message.

```
If Len(SMTP.RemoteHost) = 0 Then
   SMTP.Connect
   If Len(SMTP.RemoteHost) = 0 Then
      Exit Sub
   End If
End If
```

Now we want to check that there is a connection in place. The first line effectively checks that a connection is available. If not, it tries to make one. If this second line fails, we exit the routine.

```
Set dh = SMTP.DocInput.Headers
dh.Clear
```

With the connection up and running, we transfer the basic header details from the remote host into the dh structure—this transfers the initial connection information into the DocInput structure. We can immediately delete this information since we do not need it.

```
dh.Add "From", from.text
dh.Add "To", to.text
dh.Add "Date", date.text
dh.Add "Subject", subject.text
```

We now fill the dh variable with the correct information for this message—taken from the input edit boxes on the mail entry form. In the final program, you should include checks against an empty "To" field.

```
SMTP.SendDoc, dh, body.text
```

We now send the message header and the contents of the body edit box in one command.

```
If SMTP.ReplyCode <> 221 Then

    MsgBox "Error in SendDoc call. Message is" & SMTP.ReplyString
    Else
    MsgBox "Message sent OK"

End If
```

Finally, there is a quick check to make sure that the mail server returned the correct response code of 221. If it did not, display a message box with the error text.

And that's it! These are the basic steps required to send a mail message using the SMTP control.

Receiving mail with POP3

The SMTP protocol is great for sending mail between two machines that are both connected and ready, but if you are a dial-up client, then you need to use a mail server that can store the messages in a temporary store and send them to the client when requested by the client. This protocol is called POP3 (post office protocol).

The way that POP3 works is very similar to the SMTP protocol: there are a set of commands that are used to ask the mail server if there is any mail waiting and then, if there is mail, to download mail and delete the mail from the server. Unlike SMTP, there are just two response codes to all of the commands: "+OK" and "-ERR". The error response normally also has text lines describing the problem. The one big difference from SMTP is that POP3 uses a different TCP/IP port to transfer information—it uses port 110.

Table 6.3: *POP commands*

Command	Meaning
APOP <username> <digest>	
DELE <message number>	marks the specified message number for deletion; messages are deleted on the QUIT command
LIST	returns the number and size of messages stored on the POP server
NOOP	returns "OK" from the server if the connection is working correctly
PASS	password for the username
QUIT	disconnects from the POP server
RET <message number>	gets a copy of a particular message identified by its number; use the LIST command to get the list of message numbers
RSET	removes a delete mark from a message
STAT	asks server for the number of messages stored and their size
TOP <message number> <lines>	returns the first few lines from the top of the specified message, useful to retrieve header information
UIDL	similar to LIST but returns a unique identifier for each message
USER <username>	name of the user and his mail account on the POP server

Using the POP3 control

The ICP control includes a POP3 control that you can use to manage a POP3 session between the client and a remote mail server to read new mail. To use the control, drag the icon onto your main application form; the POP3 control is operated using a set of properties, methods and events, described below.

Figure 6.6:
*Config dialog
box for
the POP3
component.*

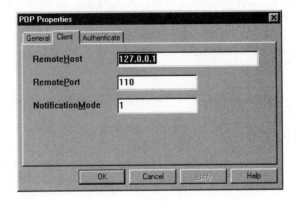

Authenticate
method

`POP3Object.Authenticate strUser, strPassword`

Should be issued once the connection has been made and before you issue any other commands—is used to authenticate the user on the remote POP3 server; if you do not supply parameters, the settings in the UserId and Password properties are used

Busy
property

`POP3Object.Busy`

Returns `True` if the control is currently executing a command (and cannot accept a new command)

Cancel
method

`POP3Object.Cancel`

Enters a request to cancel the current operation; once it has been cancelled, the Cancel event is triggered

Connect
method

`POP3Object.Connect varRemote, varRemotePort`

Establishes a connection to a remote server; if you do not supply parameters, the settings in the RemoteHost and RemotePort properties are used

Delete
method

`POP3Object.Delete intMessage`

Deletes a particular message specified by the `intMessage` number

DocOutput
property

`POP3Object.DocOutput`

Returns a handle to the `DocOutput` object that is used to read data

EnableTimer
property

`POP3Object.EnableTimer(event) = bolValue`

Controls a timer for a particular event, where event can be one of three values and the `bolValue` is `True` if the timer is enabled and `False` if it is disabled:

event = 1	TimeOut is triggered if a connection is not made in time
event = 2	TimeOut is triggered if no data arrives in the period
event = 65	TimeOut is triggered according to a user-defined event

Errors
property

`POP3Object.Errors`

Returns an error object (`icError`) that contains the last error

GetDoc
method

`POP3Object.GetDoc strURL, DocHeaders, strOutput`

Used to transfer a file from the remote mail server to the local computer; the main argument is a `DocOutput` object that is set up by the DocOutput and URL properties

strURL	string containing the name of the file on the remote host in the format "Mailto:// remotehost/filename"
DocHeaders	header information as a `DocHeaders` object
strOutput	string with the name of the file on the local machine

Last
method

`POP3Object.Last`

Returns the number of the last message accessed

**Message-
Count**
property

`POP3Object.MessageCount`

Returns the number of messages stored on the remote mail server

MessageSize
method

`POP3Object.MessageSize intMessage`

Returns the size (in bytes) of the message specified by `intMessage`

NOOP
method

`POP3Object.NOOP`

Simple command that returns a "+OK" response if the remote server is connected and running correctly

Notification- Mode property	`POP3Object.NotificationMode = intValue` Defines when notification is reported to the application where:

`intValue = 0`	notification is reported when the action has completed
`intValue = 1`	notification is reported when new data is received

Password property	`POP3Object.Password = strValue` Property that holds or returns the string value with the password for the user

Protocol- State property	`POP3Object.ProtocolState` Defines the state of the protocol being used by the control, returns one of the following four values:

integer returned	meaning
0	initial state, before a connection is established
1	authorization state, once a connection is open but before user authentication
2	transaction state, client has logged in and a full interactive link is available
3	update state, after a Quit command but before the connection has been broken (normally during message deletion)

Quit method	`POP3Object.Quit` Disconnects from the POP3 server

RemoteHost property	`POP3Object.RemoteHost = strValue` Property where `strValue` contains the URL or IP address of the remote host; use the Connect method to define and then make the connection

RemotePort property	`POP3Object.RemotePort = lngValue` Property that defines the TCP/IP port being used for the POP3 control—normally port 110

ReplyCode property	`POP3Object.ReplyCode`

Returns a long integer reply value with the last reply code generated by the POP3 mail server

ReplyString
property

`POP3Object.ReplyString`

Returns a string reply value with the last reply text generated by the POP3 mail server

Reset
method

`POP3object.Reset`

Unmarks any messages that were marked for deletion

Retrieve-Message
method

`POP3Object.RetrieveMessage intMessage, DocOutput`

Asks the remote server to send the message specified by the `intMessage` number, which is then stored in the DocOutput object

State
property

`POP3Object.State`

Returns an integer that defines the current state of the connection

integer returned	meaning
1	connecting, connection requested and waiting for acknowledgement
2	resolving host, waiting for translation of a URL to an IP address
3	host resolved, successful translation of a URL to an IP address
4	connected, connection has been established
5	disconnecting, request to disconnect
6	disconnected, no connection

TimeOut
property

`POP3Object.TimeOut(event) = lngValue`

(Used with EnableTimer property) `lngValue` contains the length of the timer period used for the specified event

`event = 1`	TimeOut is triggered if a connection is not made in time
`event = 2`	TimeOut is triggered if no data arrives in the period
`event = 65`	TimeOut is triggered according to a user-defined event

TopLines
property

```
POP3Object.TopLines = intValue
```

Sets or returns the number of lines of a message that should be displayed when a TopMessage method is executed

TopMessage
method

```
POP3Object.TopMessage intMessage, DocOutput
```

Retrieves the first few lines of a message (where the number of lines is specified by TopLines property; the output from the mail server is stored in the name DocOutput object—be sure to check that this command is supported by the server by using the TopSupported property

**TopSup-
ported**
property

```
POP3Object.TopSupported
```

Returns a True value if the remote mail server supports the TopMessage (and TOP POP3) commands

URL
property

```
POP3Object.URL = strValue
```

Contains the full name and path of the document being received or of a document requested by the DocOutput property and retrieved with the SendDoc method

UserId
property

```
POP3Object.UserId = strValue
```

Contains or returns a string with the name of the user on the remote POP3 server; see also Password

Working with the POP3 control

The POP3 control within the NetMaster's ICP suite is very simple to use, once you have established a few basic parameters. In the following section, I will show you the basic routines that you could use to connect to a remote mail server and read new mail. First, drag the POP3 control onto the main VB form and name it POP3.

The first step is to connect to the remote mail server (assuming that your dialer has set up the physical connection using a modem, ISDN or router). Your code would look like the following:

```
Private Sub Connect()
    If len(POP3.RemoteHost) = 0 Then
        POP3.Connect
    End If

    'Now free up the processor while the connection is
    'being established
```

```
        Do While (POP3.State = prcConnecting) Or (POP3.State=
         prcResolvingHost) Or (POP3.State=prcHostResolved)

            DoEvents

    Loop

    'Now check the connection is established; report error if not
    If POP3.State <> prcConnected Then

        MsgBox "Error in connecting to server. Reported Message:"
        & POP3.ReplyString

        Exit Sub
    End If

    'Now wait until the control has finished all its processing
    'and connection handshakes
    Do While POP3.Busy
        DoEvents
    Loop

    'Now, send the user authentication details stored in the
    'property sheet
    POP3.Authenticate

    'Now wait until the user has been cleared
    Do While POP3.Busy
        DoEvents
    Loop

    'Now check that the user was accepted and cleared
    If (POP3.ReplyCode <> 0 ) Then
    MsgBox "Error in user authenticate. Reported Message:"
        & POP3.ReplyString
    End If

    'Now we are sure we are connected, check message status
    MailWaiting = POP3.MessageCount
End Sub
```

Figure 6.7:
*The form for
our mail
reader lists
header on the
left, with
details on the
right.*

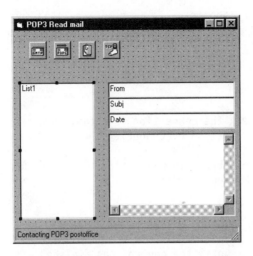

Working with DocOutput: Managing POP3 message information

The best—and the most difficult—part of the POP3 control is the way in which it will pass all information to a named DocOutput routine for processing. This means that you can build your own routine to determine how you want to filter the message data as it arrives from the mail server. It also means that the routines to strip out the To:, From:, and Subject: lines of the message header are all in a central routine that is called automatically by the ActiveX routine as it reads a message.

Table 6.4: *DocOutput.State values*

Value	Constant	Meaning
0	icDocNone	no transfer in progress
1	icDocBegin	transfer initiated
2	icDocHeaders	headers are being transferred
3	icDocData	data is available
4	icDocError	error has occurred
5	icDocEnd	transfer complete

The second advantage of the DocOutput routine is that you can define the output form details within this processing routine so that the new message information is displayed in the correct form as it arrives and without any further program intervention.

The DocOutput routine is normally a series of Case statements that work according to the setting of the DocOutput.State object condition, described in Table 6.4.

This allows your DocOutput processing routine to switch to the correct routine according to the value of the State property.

```
Dim dh As DocHeader
Dim varData As Variant
Select Case DocOutput.State
```

These first three lines define an object called "dh" that has the same structure as the DocHeader library object and will contain the header information, if the DocOutput.State indicates that headers are being transferred. The second line defines a Variant data type called varData that will hold the message data when it's available. The third line simply starts the Select-Case statement that is the central control of this routine.

```
Case icDocBegin
'clear the buffers or screen display forms
```

This first Case statement is, in this case, empty. If you have a form displayed with a edit box for the mail header and another for the mail text, then you could use this section to clear these boxes since there is a new transfer about to start.

```
Case icDocHeaders

    'receiving header information, so split up the header data
    For each dh In DocOutput.Headers

        Select Case dh.Name
        Case "Subject"
            subject(1) = dh.value
        Case "From"
            subject(2) = dh.value
        Case "Date"
            subject(3) = dh.value
        End Select

    Next dh
```

In this second Case statement, we are picking up the header information from the message. This header information is picked out of the DocOuput.Headers data stream using the DocHeader structure (our dh variable is an instance of this type of structure). We skip through the data stream len(dh) bytes at a time and then do a nested Select–Case statement on the resulting data to look at the two parts of the Doc-Header structure: the Name (the part of the header) and the value (the actual information). These parts are separated into the first three locations of an array you could include more header information, such as the CC fields and more.

```
Case icDocData
    DocOutput.GetData varData
    'store the message data into a form edit control here
```

In this Case statement, we are extracting the message data into a variant data type called varData. This data can then be stored directly into an edit box or note box control on a form.

```
Case icDocError
    MsgBox "DocOutput Error"
```

Our last Case statement pops up a warning dialog that there has been an error. This should, ideally, point to a more sophisticated error routine that picks up the mail server error message (using POP3.Reply-Code) and either acts on this or converts it to a nice user-friendly message.

Conclusion

The importance of SMTP and POP3 for mail delivery has rocketed with the Internet and as intranets are installed across the corporate world. As this chapter shows, these two TCP/IP protocols are relatively easy to use and allow a developer to create a powerful email system that does not have the wide-area network limitations of MAPI and can bridge just about any network system.

7

Multiuser Network Database Mechanics

Introduction

Visual Basic is an ideal tool to use when creating a database application or a front-end to a database server. Included with Visual Basic is support for the Jet engine (used by Microsoft Access) together with ODBC drivers to access "foreign" format databases.

If you are creating a database application that will be used by several users on a network or a standalone application that accesses a shared database file, you need to understand how to provide controls over the way the data is used, shared and updated to prevent problems caused when several users try to update the same table at the same time.

In this chapter, I cover many of the aspects of multiuser programming, including database design that will ensure that databases are shared safely.

Multiuser access to a database

One of the classic examples of the problems that you will encounter when programming for multiuser installations on a network is that of multiuser access to a single database. Each user runs a standalone VB application on their computer but the application links to a shared copy of a database file stored on a file server.

By default, the Microsoft Jet engine is clever enough to cope with multiple users and will automatically add record locking to prevent one user updating a record that another user is reading. However, there are a range of techniques to get the most out of this system.

Opening a database for exclusive use

To allow a user to open a database for exclusive use, preventing any other user from accessing the shared database, you can use one of the command line parameters in the OpenDatabase function within the Jet command set. The command would look like this:

```
Set db = DBEngine.Workspaces(0).OpenDatabase(dbName, bolExclusive)
```

You should set bolExclusive to True if you want to open the database exclusively or False for general operation. If you execute this function there is always the possibility that another user on the network has just opened the database in exclusive mode, denying you the chance of doing so. To get around this you need to trap any error generated by this function. The function would return an error code of 3356 if the file is already open exclusively. The code to do this would look like this:

```
On Error Goto ErrorHandle

Set db = DBEngine.Workspaces(0).OpenDatabase(dbName, bolExclusive)

ErrorHandle:
    If Err.Number = 3356 Then
        'database is already opened exclusively
        MsgBox "Database is already open!"
    End If
```

Figure 7.1:
Trapping database warnings.

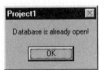

In fact, you could link this error message to some of the API network functions mentioned earlier in this book to see who is using the shared resource and even send an email requesting time on the database!

Opening a table for exclusive use

When you open a table, or recordset, you normally have the usual Jet record locking protection, but this is not always enough if you want to update a set of records without being disturbed by other users. The way around this is to open the recordset using its locking parameter to define the extra level of security that you want to implement.

The extra locking security is based on the OpenRecordset method that is one of the standard Jet commands. It allows you to prevent other users from even viewing the table during your access time or, less brutally, to allow other users to view the table but not add or change the data in the table. (This latter restriction can also be applied to a Dynaset or Snapshot; the former only applies to tables.) If another user now tries to open the same table that you have just locked, they will be greeted by an error 3261 from the Jet engine, which must be trapped.

The code to open the database, then open the "Contacts" table from the database in locked mode, is described below:

```
'open database
Set db = DBEngine.Workspace(0).OpenDatabase(dbName)
'now open table Contacts with permission set by intAccess
Set rs = db.OpenRecordset("Contacts", dbOpenTable, intAccess)
'set the index for the table
rs.Index = "PrimaryKey"
'tell Jet to free up any unused index locks
DBEngine.Idle dbFreeLocks

ErrorHandle:
 If Err.Number = 3261
    'another user has opened the table with either deny read
    'or deny write and so locked the table
    'should now try to open in read-only mode to see if this is
    'possible - then resume and try again
    intAccess = dbReadOnly
    Resume
 End If
```

This routine has a number of new sections of code that are worth covering. The first is the intAccess variable that defines the way you want to open the table. If you set intAccess equal to the dbDenyRead constant, you will open the table and prevent any other user being able to read the table. If you set intAccess equal to dbDenyWrite, other users will be able to open the file in read-only mode.

The next part of the code is the ErrorHandle handler. This traps the error 3261 that is generated when the user tries to open the table for normal access and another user has already opened the table with either dbDenyRead or dbDenyWrite. At this stage, you know that the table has been protected, but you are not sure to what level. The best solution is to ask the user if they want to try to open the table in Read Only mode. Try this (all within the error handler) and test for an error. If there is an error, the table was opened by the other user in dbDenyRead mode. If there was no error, the other user opened the table in dbDenyWrite mode and you are now able to view it in read-only mode.

The final point worth noting is a trick to force the Jet engine into releasing any locks on the table's index. The problem stems from the fact that any application needs to lock the index to read-only mode for other users while it is using the index. Jet copes with this automatically, but sometimes these locks get stuck and an error message is generated. The Idle method explicitly tells Jet to drop unwanted locks on the index.

Working with record locking

The Jet engine allows multiple concurrent users to access shared data records by implementing a system of locking records. However, unlike many other databases, Jet doesn't lock an individual record; instead it locks a 2K (2048 bytes) page of records. The advantage of this page locking scheme is that there's less overhead and so improved performance over true record locking. The downside is that Jet will usually lock more records than you would like (which becomes more important when using pessimistic locking in which a user can lock a record for a long period of time). There are three basic ways of providing locks to a recordset in a multiuser environment:

1. **No Locks** (called *optimistic locking*)

   This is the default setting for Jet. In this situation, the page of records that contains the currently edited record is locked only during the instant when the record is being saved—it is not locked during editing.

   advantages of using *optimistic* locking are:

   - simple to use
   - unlikely to lock other users out of records
   - better performance than pessimistic locking

   disadvantages of using *optimistic* locking are:

   - a user can overwrite another user's edits

2. **Edited Record** (called *pessimistic locking*)

   In this scheme, the page containing the record is locked as soon as a user begins to edit the record.

   advantages of *pessimistic* locking are:

- simple to implement
- prevents users from overwriting each other's work
- ideal for a workgroup where users are unlikely to be editing the same record

disadvantages of *pessimistic* locking are:

- usually locks multiple records
- if a user is at the end of a table, other users may be prevented from adding new records because he has locked the last page
- not recommended for a system in which users edit the same records or where lots of users add new records at the same time

3. **All Records**

This setting locks all records in the entire recordset; this is only really useful when carrying out a batch update or maintenance on a table.

For most applications, optimistic locking can be the better scheme since it does not prevent users from being able to edit or add records for a long period of time, which is the problem of pessimistic locking. At least with optimistic locking you can display a write-conflict message and allow the user to deal with this simpler problem. If you do select pessimistic locking, you need to ensure that your VB application detects the conflict errors and deals with them smartly.

Using record locking

To work with record locking in your VB code you need to set the LockEdits property of the data control (or recordset object) in your application. For example:

```
Data1.RecordSet.LockEdits = True   'sets pessimistic locking
Data1.RecordSet.LockEdits = False  'sets optimistic locking
```

As I mentioned above, the problem with both types of locking—particularly pessimistic locking—is that any lock errors should be spotted and dealt with as soon as possible. To do this, you need to build in an error handling routine that traps any error by using the Error event of the data control. Your error code needs to manage the following errors.

Table 7.1: *Pessimistic locking errors*

Error code	Reason
3197	Data has changed; operation stopped. Usually occurs when you try to read a record that has been updated or deleted since you last refreshed the dataset.
3260	Record is currently locked by user username on machine machinename. Usually occurs when you attempt to edit a record that is currently locked by another user.

Table 7.2: *Optimistic locking errors*

Error code	Reason
3186	Couldn't save; record you are trying to update is currently locked by user username on machine machinename.
3197	Data has changed; operation stopped. Usually occurs when you try to read a record that has been updated or deleted since you last refreshed the dataset.
3260	Record is currently locked by user username on machine machinename. Usually occurs when you attempt to edit a record that is currently locked by another user.

Locking a particular record

If you want to lock an individual record within Jet you will need to use a little cunning! You can force Jet to lock an individual record by ensuring that the record is bigger than half a page (1024 bytes). This works because Jet will not store a new record on a partially filled page if it can't fit the entire record on that page. When calculating the size of a record, don't forget that memo and OLE objects are not stored within the main record so just count the size of their address pointers.

Transaction processing

Using transaction processing can dramatically change the security and reliability of your multiuser database. In a transaction processing scheme, a number of related actions are grouped together into one unit. A transaction succeeds if all the actions in this unit succeed; otherwise, the transaction fails and the database is not updated by the unit of actions.

Jet allows you to work with transaction processing using a few basic methods to the data control. BeginTrans, CommitTrans, and Rollback methods are the three controls that can be used with the Workspace object. BeginTrans defines the start of the operations that are a transaction; CommitTrans executes the transaction and writes to disk; Rollback is used to undo the changes of CommitTrans.

All three transaction statements work on the default workspace Workspaces(0); Jet will honor your locking method when carrying out a transaction, so pessimistic and optimistic locks still work. If Jet encounters a locked record during a transaction you will see the same error returns as described above. You should then rollback the transaction and try again.

Minimizing network traffic with databases

In the usual course of events, an Access database (that is, a native format database used by Jet) contains all the code within a single file—including the data, reports, queries, macros and so on. For example, if you designed and manage the database using Access itself and your users update the data using VB, then all your forms and queries are in the database file. If a user is trying to access an object within this database, the entire file has to be sent over the network, causing a lot of unnecessary traffic.

The way to reduce network traffic is to split the database so that just the minimum data files are stored in the shared database file on the file server. Your admin workstation would then have an application database with a local database file full of the forms, queries and so on—and an attachment to the shared database.

Database security

The Jet engine allows a developer to implement user- and group-based security, independent of any other network security. This prompts users for their name and password before allowing them access to the data. However, the current Access security measures are not the world's best and there is plenty of debate and tricks on how to improve this system—check the CompuServe forums and newsgroups for more details.

To set up and define the initial security levels, you need to use Access—you cannot currently use VB to set up the security. Installing security means creating a SYSTEM.MDW (called SYSTEM.MDA in 16-bit installations) file that holds the security profiles for the database. One of the main problems of this security system is that if you decide to remove the pointer to the SYSTEM file from the Windows INI file then there are no security checks!

Figure 7.2:
*The Jet engine
allows a
developer to
define user
and group
permissions.*

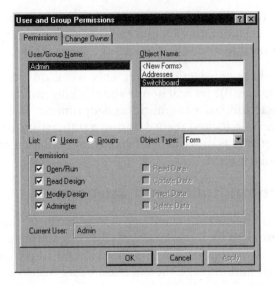

However, if you do decide to use the security features of Access/Jet, you can log in to a session using the DefaultUser and DefaultPassword properties to the database component.

Remote data controls

So far in this chapter, the information has centered around the Jet database engine and—naturally—the VB data control. These controls can access a shared database file and do so by using the DAO to connect to the ODBC driver manager.

The second method of reaching remote, shared data is to use the RemoteData control; the main difference from the standard data control is that this uses the RDO to connect to the ODBC driver manager. Although both systems use the same ODBC manager, the two engines cannot share objects or resources. There are a couple of other caveats in using the RemoteData control: first, you need to install the control into the VB toolbox; secondly, you can only use this with 32-bit systems.

Using the remote data controls gives the developer better control over the way database access and control is carried out over a network. However, since this control and its properties are well documented in the help files and manual, I will refer you to these books for further information.

Conclusion

This chapter provides a basic introduction to the problems and solutions of managing data access in a multiuser environment over a network. The controls originally supplied by Microsoft and now sourced from NetMasters allow the developer to ensure that data is never corrupted by another user and that two users cannot try to update the same information at the same time.

Perhaps the most important part of a multiuser database application is its error-trapping routines. Although there are only three basic errors to manage, you do need to ensure that these are dealt with correctly and as early as possible. If you do not, your users will be faced with confusing error message boxes!

8

TCP/IP and
Socket Programming

Introduction

The Internet has become vitally important for almost all businesses and is used for a very wide variety of applications. Some companies use it as a virtual telephone or video conferencing system, others use it for research, sales or delivering product. Almost everybody uses the Internet for electronic mail.

There are now thousands of commercial applications that work with the Internet. For example, there are dozens of email front-ends that provide different user interfaces to the same email protocol. Other applications are used to transfer files, access search engines to find information on the Web, or view messages on a public newsgroup.

Many of these applications are shareware and provide an excellent set of features but without the particular function you are looking for. If you are a company developer, you might prefer a commercial application with support, but cannot find one that provides the features. Alternatively, you might not like the way controls in an application work and would rather tailor these to your own use.

The Internet and Visual Basic

Visual Basic provides a great platform to solve almost any Internet application problem. It is very easy to create your own applications that look and work just the way you or your company likes. There is no real compromise on features, since a VB Internet application can provide all the features of most of the applications already available. For example, you can easily create an Internet email application, Web browser, file transfer utility, or newsgroup reader.

Where VB really starts to score is that you can create applications that integrate Internet functions within an existing application and hide the Internet from your users! For example, it's easy to create an email application that, to the user, looks the same but gives them the choice of sending internal email using MAPI (see Chapter 5) or Internet mail.

Figure 8.1:
An HTML
browser with
four elements.

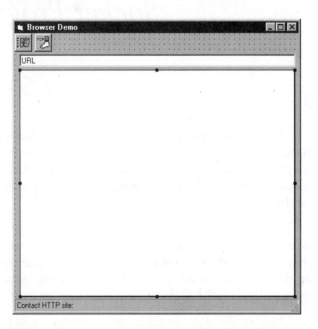

Another perfect VB application is a standalone reasearch application that uses the Internet to get up-to-date information and then presents this to the user in a simple format. For example, you can build a stock price monitor that accesses a stock price Web site every hour and pulls off the current price of selected stocks; it can then display these as a graph on-screen or send the user an email if there's a sudden price change. Visual Basic is just as good for intranet applications where the company runs an internal web; you can create a Web browser by dropping an HTML viewer control onto your VB form—you can then add any extra controls you need. If you do not want to scare your users with the complex commercial Web browsers currently available, create the simplest HTML viewer with VB.

Accessing the Internet

To construct a VB application that can provide access to the Internet, you need a number of items before you can get up and running:

- account with an ISP (Internet service provider) or an intranet
- dial-in software with Winsock to access the service (such as Windows Internet Dial)
- Internet control for VB (such as the NetMasters Internet Control Pack)

The Internet control for VB provides the high-end functions and usually links to the Internet using the Winsock DLL; this DLL in turn links to a dialer that actually dials the access telephone or ISDN number, logs in and makes a connection with the ISP. Some ISPs provide a starter kit with all these features; otherwise, you can use the built-in dialer and Winsock that's part of Windows 95. If you have a main router linking your company LAN to the Internet, you will still have a Winsock DLL with a redirector that points to the router rather than a modem.

Figure 8.2:
Adding the NetMasters HTTP component.

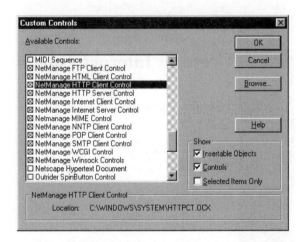

If your version of VB does not have a set of Internet controls (sometimes called TCP/IP controls) then you can download a trial version of one of the many third-party controls from their Web site, or you can download the NetMasters ICP (Internet Control Pack)—previously known as the Microsoft ICP—from its Web site. Here are some of the useful sites:

```
www.netmasters.com
www.apiary.com
www.progress.com/crescent
```

In this chapter, I will be using the NetMasters suite of Internet controls, called the Internet Control Pack, which provides a range of functions to allow a VB application to establish a TCP/IP session, transfer email using SMTP/POP3 protocols, display HTML Web pages, transfer data using FTP and more! This suite used to be supplied by Microsoft, but has recently changed to NetMasters. These controls are bundled together as a 32-bit ActiveX control, which is great if you are using one of the newer versions of Visual Basic and running the applications under Windows 95 or NT, but is not so good if you are using a flavor of VB that only supports 16-bit VBX library extensions. In this latter case, I would suggest that you look at the demo versions of the VBX libraries available from Aviary and Crescent and see if these provide the functions that you require (these libraries are also available as OCX and ActiveX controls for 32-bit development).

Figure 8.3:
Other Internet component suites are available for developers.

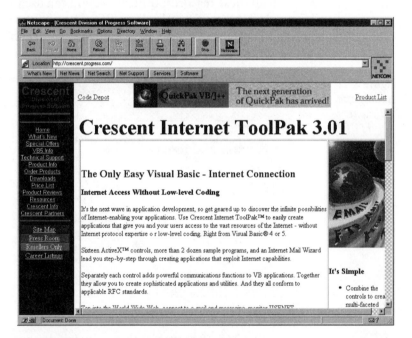

TCP/IP basics for your server

One of the most important technical issues that you must understand before you can achieve anything on the Internet is TCP/IP (transmission control protocol/Internet procol). TCP/IP actually refers to a group of protocols that are used for data transmission; it is the communications protocol used in most Unix networks, the Internet, and as a safe neutral protocol in many mixed-platform networks.

TCP/IP was developed in 1973 but was not published as a standard until 1983, when it was chosen as the standard protocol for communications over the new ARPAnet wide area network (an early forerunner of the Internet). One of the reasons for TCP/IP's popularity in academic networks and within Unix stems from its origins in the University of California, Berkeley, which developed the BSD series of Unix products, each incorporating the new TCP/IP protocol.

TCP/IP is used because it has a number of very important benefits:

- it will run on a wide range of hardware, including Ethernet, Token Ring, and X.25
- it will work on different computer platforms and operating systems, including Macintosh, Unix, PC, mainframe and PDA
- it is an open standard that is not owned by any manufacturer
- it has a standard method of addressing that can uniquely identify each host on a vast network such as the Internet
- it can route data via a particular route to reduce traffic or to bypass a faulty link

The TCP/IP protocol has five layers and can be closely modeled to the ISO/OSI seven-layer network model.

As a data packet passes from the application layer down through the layers, each layer adds its own header and footer information before passing the new packet down to the next layer. Once at the physical layer, the complete packet is transmitted to the next node, where it is passed up the layers with the information headers stripped off one by one. At the end, the data packet arrives at the application layer of the destination.

These packets of information that are passed over the network are called datagrams; each datagram contains a header that includes all the relevant information needed to deliver the datagram correctly. The main parts of the datagram header include the source and destination port numbers that are used to send the data to be transferred between the correct processes running on each computer. There is also a sequence number that allows the destination computer to rebuild the sequence of datagrams into the correct order and, lastly, there is an error-detection checksum.

Figure 8.4: *You'll need two components for a conversation with a Web server.*

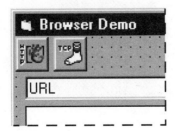

The **Internet protocol** (IP) part of the complete TCP/IP family is responsible for moving the data from one computer to another using the network layer of the model. The IP is limited in that it does not contain any error detection or correction information, nor does it establish or manage the link. Instead, it relies on TCP to carry out all of these functions—the IP simply sends the datagram. As with the other layers, IP adds its own header to the datagram it receives. This header contains basic information such as the length of the data, protocol, and version of IP being used. (Currently, IP version 4 is in common use.)

Working on top of the TCP/IP suite of protocols are all sorts of applications that will be familiar to most readers: SNMP for network management, FTP for file transfers, SMTP for email transfer, and Telnet to remotely log in to a server.

TCP/IP at work

Within a network that is using the TCP/IP suite of protocols there are two terms that often confuse new users: ports and sockets.

Whenever data is transferred from one application to another, it technically is being transferred from one port to another port on the destination computer: the port number is used to identify the application that is running on a computer. When the TCP/IP protocol receives data, it tries to identify the correct port number based on the type of data using a look-up table.

The port number is a 16-bit number in the range 1–32767; some port numbers are used, by convention, for particular applications. For example, a Web server application is almost always on port 80, and a Telnet server application is almost always on port 23.

Figure 8.5:
Configuring the basic TCP port used for an HTTP conversation.

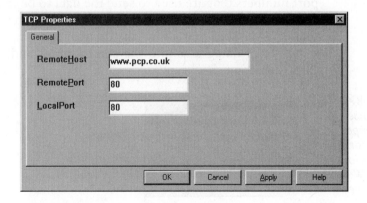

A *socket* identifies a particular networking session by combining the IP address and the port address; for any network session there are always two sockets defined—one for the source and one for the destination. Together they form a complete networking unit.

IP addressing

The IP (Internet protocol) actually moves a datagram between two computers, from the source port to the destination port (both identified in the datagram header). In addition to this way of identifying the application that is sending or receiving the datagram, IP must also be able to identify the correct computers in the transfer.

In order to identify each computer on the network, each different computer (or host) is allocated a unique IP address. These 32-bit numbers are normally written as four eight-bit byte values (called octets), each separated by a full-stop (for example, 123.222.3.44).

Within the IP address, the highest two bytes (the first two on the left) define the network address, and the lowest two bytes (the last two on the right) define the host address of a particular computer on the network. Two special host addresses are reserved: in order to identify the network address, a complete address with the host address set to zero is used, for example, "44.0.0.0" identifies the network address as 44. A complete address with the host address part set to 255 (all bits set) is used to broadcast to all hosts on the network, for example, any data sent to the address "44.5.255.255" is broadcast to all hosts on the "44.5" network.

Host names

One of the disadvantages of an IP address is that, even when written in the four-part, dotted-decimal format, it is still difficult to remember. Instead, the Internet uses host names that are associated with an IP address. Normally, these are written as the domain name followed by the host name within that domain. For example, "www.mycompany.com" has a domain name of "www" and a host name of "mycompany.com". The entire three-word name is sometimes called a *fully qualified host name* and refers to a host with a particular, unique IP address.

Accessing host names

The advantage of using a host name instead of a dotted-decimal format IP address is that it's easy for a user to remember. The disadvantage is that somewhere on the Internet there needs to be a table that will translate any host name into its IP address. This is called a DNS (domain name service) server, which can hold every IP address on the Internet and its corresponding name.

The system works as follows: if a user types in a full URL to a Web site in his or her Web browser, such as "http://www.mycompany.com", then the browser will pass this host name on to the TCP/IP protocol and ask it if it knows this name. If it does not (normally anything other than the local name) then TCP/IP will pass the name on to the nearest DNS server and ask it for the correct IP address. This address is retrieved and passed back to the browser, which can then make the connection.

TCP/IP with Microsoft

Originally, TCP/IP was developed for a Unix environment. When linking a Microsoft operating system (such as Windows) with its default NetBEUI protocol to the Internet and its default TCP/IP protocol, there has to be a bridge between the two systems.

NetBEUI is based on the NetBIOS protocol and is generally used for most Microsoft networks. The problems start when you try to install TCP/IP on a Microsoft network that was previously set up with Net-BEUI. For example, under NetBEUI you can define a LAN printer server with a text name, such as Laser1. Try to find this print server using TCP/IP and it'll come up blank—it doesn't know about text names. To get around this, Microsoft developed WINS (Windows Internet naming service) as a way of mapping NetBEUI names to IP addresses.

If you want to link your Web server to your office LAN and share resources between the two, you will find it far easier to install WINS so that you can still refer to network resources by their NetBEUI names. Once installed, WINS will find out the various addresses and names of nodes that are connected to the network. As users switch their workstations on and off, WINS will automatically modify its data file of mappings.

Of course, if you are not connected to a Windows network or do not need to share NetBEUI network resources, then you do not need to set up the WINS service.

Testing an IP address

The Internet has a standard utility that lets you test any route or host or other computer on the Internet to make sure that it is working correctly. This is called a PING (packet Internet groper) and will send a diagnostic packet to the named IP address; if the destination address receives the diagnostic packet, it must respond with an acknowledgement and this is then displayed as a result from PING.

For example, if you have set up a new Internet server and want to check that it is working correctly, you can use PING to send a loopback test to your own server. If all is working correctly, this will report back the time taken for the acknowledgement from your own server to be displayed and you will see a correct reply response. To carry out this test, use:

```
PING 127.0.0.1
```

If there is a problem somewhere with the server configuration, there will be a timeout and no acknowledgement will be generated.

Figure 8.6:
A PING utility
helps test a
connection.

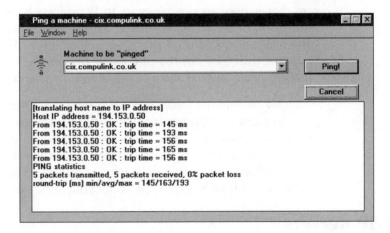

You can also use PING to test your gateway setup between your Web server and the Internet. For example, if you are working on your server and want to test the Internet gateway, send a PING command to an external host, either your ISP's host name or another server site such as "www.ibm.com" and wait to see the response. If there is a timeout or no response, it could mean that your gateway is not working or that the destination host is very, very busy.

An overview of DNS

A domain name service (DNS) server is responsible for storing details about how to locate hosts, how to route email and how to find the local gateway. The domain name system maps out every domain and host within the Internet and is vast. Each DNS server is responsible for one part of the entire map and might just hold information about its own domain or might hold information about a number of domains.

The best way to visualize the domain name system is using a tree map (rather similar to the old tree maps for a DOS or Unix directory structure). At the top of the tree is the root. Beneath this are branches for the types of host: .com, .edu, .gov, .net and so on. Beneath each of these classifications are further branches that include the domain names for each host, such as "mycompany" and under each host are branches for the services this host offers, such as "www," email and FTP. The complete domain name for a host is created by reading from the bottom up: "www.mycompany.com".

There is another branch from the root within the domain name system that is used to reverse-map an IP address back to a text domain name. This branch is called "arpa" and beneath it is another sub-branch called "in-addr." Beneath this is a tree four layers deep that completely maps the four bytes of the full 32-bit IP address. This feature is called "in-addr.arpa" and is used by DNS servers to retrieve a host name.

Lastly, within the domain name system there are root name servers. Each of these computers is responsible for the names within its category: .com, .edu, .net, .gov and so on. The root computers hold lists of all the hosts in their category together with the relevant IP address. In turn, one level down, each host (that is, a Web server) has a DNS server that holds address information about your server and setup.

TCP/IP servers

The TCP/IP protocol has several standard applications that provide services over the Internet. Each uses its own standard language to send and receive information over the Net. The applications are known to users as features such as the World Wide Web, email, file transfer and newsgroups, but in fact each of these is an example of a TCP/IP application and each has its own protocol. In this chapter I will describe each of the main protocols and its application:

- electronic mail—SMTP/POP3
- World Wide Web—HTTP
- newsgroups—NNTP
- file transfer—FTP

Figure 8.7:
*A Visual Basic
application
that merges
email with an
email mailing
list.*

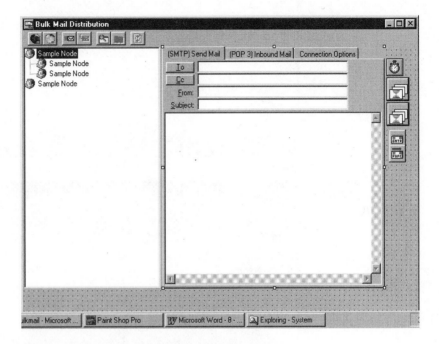

Figure 8.8:
*An enhanced
Web browser.*

Figure 8.9:
The NNTP
newsreader
application.

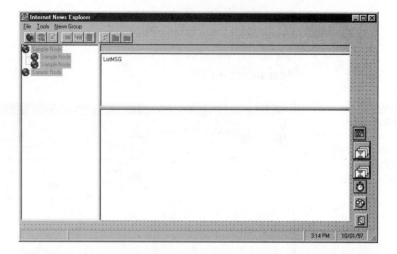

Figure 8.10:
An FTP utility
in Visual Basic
design mode.

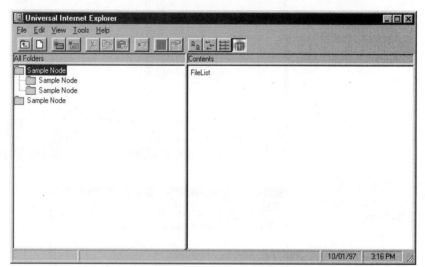

Client–Server: Transferring data over TCP/IP

So far in this book, you have seen how to send and receive email messages using the pair of official mail protocols, SMTP and POP3. However, if you are connected to another computer via a network that uses the TCP/IP protocol you can do much more. One of the features of TCP/IP that was briefly described at the start of this chapter is sockets, which provide a way for two applications to communicate over a TCP/IP network.

In general, this control would normally be used as another way of transferring information to a TCP/IP server, such as an HTTP or FTP server, but it can work equally as well to allow a two-way conversation between your own client and server programs. Once the two applications create a connection and define a socket layer link, each can send a stream of data—or just individual bytes—to the other listening application. Since this works over any network, you can create a distributed system using a WAN, such as the Internet, to allow a sales order application to connect to a stock control application in a remote warehouse.

A *socket* is a channel between two objects on a network and is maintained under Windows using a Winsock tool (Windows Sockets). Luckily, Visual Basic 5 includes a Winsock control, but there are plenty of third-party control libraries that work as VBX, OCX or ActiveX controls for 16- or 32-bit development.

Any conversation between two applications is called a *client–server exchange*. The client application contacts the server application, which is listening for a client. Once the connection has been made, either application can send or receive data. The full connection process is as follows.

Client application:

- To create a connection you need the server's address (or IP address) to feed into the RemoteHost property and the port its listening on to set the RemotePort property
- Now start the Connect method

Server application:

- Sets a TCP/IP port on which to listen for client (using the LocalPort property)
- Start the Listen method
- When the client requests a connection, the ConnectionRequest event is fired
- Start the Accept method to complete the connection

Blocking and nonblocking sockets

As you start to experiment with sockets, you will soon discover that there are two types of socket: blocking and nonblocking. These two methods relate to the way that control of the socket is handled when it is busy with another job. For example, if you are writing a client application and perform a read operation, you will have to wait until the server sends data out before the client read operation can complete naturally.

To allow the client to complete there are two ways of progressing: either wait until the data arrives and return the data or return immediately with an error message. The first option is called a *blocking* socket (because it blocks all other operation until it completes) and the second is called a *nonblocking* socket.

If your client application uses a nonblocking socket, you will need another system that can read the data. Here again, there are two options. The first is to poll the port that checks the port regularly to see if any data has arrived (and is driven by a timer); the second method is to use a notifier event. In this latter method, the program is notified that data has arrived by the status of an event flag—the process is called *asynchronous notification* and is the preferred method of handling nonblocking socket data transfers.

Client application properties and methods

RemoteHost
property

`TCP.RemoteHost = strValue`

Lets you set the name of the remote computer to which you want to make a connection; the strValue argument contains the name of the remote computer either as a UNC name (e.g. FTP://ftp.microsoft.com) or as an IP address

RemotePort
property

`TCP.RemotePort = lngPort`

Defines the port that the client should use to contact the server computer; the default is port 80, which is normally used for HTTP (Web page) transfers, but this could equally be 21 for FTP or any other port for custom data transfers

Connect
method

`TCP.Connect remoteHost, remotePort`

Requests a connection to a remote host using the remote port defined; if the parameters are not included in this command, the RemoteHost and RemotePort properties are used

Server application properties and methods

LocalPort
property

`TCP.LocalPort = lngPort`

Defines the port that the server should listen on for any client computer

Listen method	`TCP.Listen`
	Creates a server socket and sets the process to listen for a client on the specified port

Connection-Request event	`TCP_ConnectionRequest(lngRequestID As Long)`
	Event that is triggered when the server application receives a request for a connection from a client

Accept method	`TCP.Accept lngRequestID`
	Used to accept an incoming connection once alerted by the ConnectionRequest event (which also provides the `lngReqestID` handle)

Data transfer properties and methods

DataArrival event	`TCP_DataArrival(byteTotal As Long)`
	Event that is triggered when new data is received by the control; also provides the `byteTotal` count of how much data is available (the alternative is to use the BytesReceived property)

BytesReceived property	`TCP.BytesReceived`
	Returns the amount of new data that has been received and is waiting in the receive buffer; this can now be read using the GetData method

GetData method	`TCP.GetData Data, Type, MaxLen`
	Retrieves the data from the receive buffer. Normally you would link this to the DataArrival event and try to retrieve all the new data in one operation; if you do not, the remaining data will probably be lost (an error 10040 will be generated to warn of data loss). You can specify the type of data that you are retrieving, but this is an optional argument

SendData method	`TCP.SendData Data`
	Used to send data to the port

Send-Progress event	`TCP_SendProgress(bytesSent As Long, bytesRemaining As Long)`
	This event reports on the amount of data that has been sent and the amount still left in the buffer waiting to be sent

SendComplete event	`TCP_SendComplete`
	Event that is triggered when all the data has been sent

Programming a client–server application

Using the methods, properties and events listed above, it is now possible to create a simple client–server application that will transfer data between two applications.

The server application

The server starts by listening on port 500, then accepting a client request; this acceptance is triggered by the ConnectionRequest event. The server will only stop working when the client initiates the closing operation. The other routines in the server application work as a simple response mechanism to any received data: the data is received from the client and displayed in an edit box on the server form, then the data string "Thank you" is returned to the client. These routines are triggered from the DataArrival event.

```
Sub Form_Load()

    'define the port to listen on
    TCP.LocalPort = 500
    TCP.Listen

    'now crude device to spend time until client closes connection
    Do While TCP.State <> sckClosing
        DoEvents
    Loop

End Sub

Private Sub TCP_Connect(requestID As Long)

    'test connection to see if it is already open - if it
    'is then close it
    If TCP.State <> sckClosed Then TCP.Close

    'accept new socket connection
    TCP.Accept requestID

End Sub

Private TCP_DataArrival(ByVal byteTotal As Long)

    Dim newData As String
    TCP.GetData newData
    Status.Text = "Total received" & Format(TCP.BytesReceived)
    Note.Text = newData
```

```
'now echo this data back to the client
newData = "Thank you"
TCP.SendData newData
```

End Sub

The client application

The client works in a rather similar way to the server, but does not hang so many of its core routines from events—instead the data is sent when the user clicks on a Send button (Command1), and the response from the server is displayed automatically in the Response edit field.

```
Sub Form_Load()

    'define the port and the remote computer's IP address
    TCP.RemotePort = 500
    TCP.RemoteHost = "212.122.22.22"
    TCP.Connect

End Sub

Sub Command1_Click()

    'when user presses the Send button on the form, send the data
    If TCP.State = sckConnected Then
        TCP.SendData Note.Text
        Do While TCP.State <> sckSendComplete
            DoEvents
        Loop
    End If

End Sub

Private TCP_DataArrival(ByVal byteTotal As Long)

    Dim newData As String
    'This will display the Thank You response from the server
    TCP.GetData newData
    Status.Text = "Total received" & Format(TCP.BytesReceived)
    Reply.Text = newData

End Sub
```

Figure 8.11:
*The client side
of our simple
client–server
utility.*

Accessing the WWW: The HTTP client

Perhaps the most user-friendly part of any Internet or intranet system is the Web pages. If you have an intranet, delivering your company's data via formatted Web pages is an excellent way of ensuring that all users see the same data. However, although you could install a full Web browser on each user's computer, you can integrate browsing features into your VB application using either the NetMasters control or similar controls from third-party developers.

The language used to describe the formatting, text, and graphics in Web pages is called *hypertext markup language* (HTML), and this type of data is delivered to a client by the HTTP TCP/IP server. To provide the functions required to access and view a Web page, you need two controls: an HTTP client control to request the Web page data from the remote server, and an HTML control to decode the HTML formatting and display the pages.

The HTTP control is very similar to both the basic sockets control (above) and the email control (earlier in this chapter). It uses similar socket commands to get data from the remote HTTP server and stores this data in a DocOutput structure, similar to the email client.

The process of requesting a Web page follows this pattern: set the URL (the HTTP server will resolve this into its correct IP address), and get the document. As a simple utility, that's it! Sure, you can add timeout traps to stop the utility waiting forever for a Web page, together with status information to tell the user how the request is progressing.

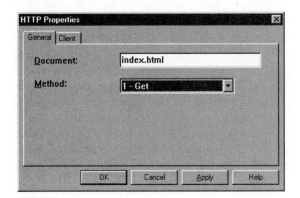

```
HTTP1.UTL = URLEntry.Text
HTTP1.GetDoc
```

Now we need an event handler to manage the incoming data that is stored in the DocOutput structure. The routine below responds to the DocOutput event that indicates that data is arriving.

```
Private Sub HTTP1_DocOutput(ByVal DocOutput As DocOutput)

   Select Case DocOutput.State

   Case icDocHeaders
   'header management routine here in cases where
   'you want to display or filter on headers

   Case icDocBegin
   HTML.Clear
   'new document, so clear fields

   Case icDocEnd
   Status.Text = "Document Done"
   'document finished

   Case icDocData
   DocOutput.GetData varData

   Case icDocError
   MsgBox "Error" & HTTP1.ReplyCode

   End Select

End Sub
```

The HTML page display control integrates many of the HTTP functions directly into its own control and allows you to create a very simple HTTP client that can display the HTML code returned by the remote HTTP server.

```
Sub Form_Load()

    HTML1.Cancel

End Sub

Sub Command1_Click()

    HTML1.RequestDoc strURL.Text

End Sub
```

Figure 8.13:
The Web browser in action with a local HTML page.

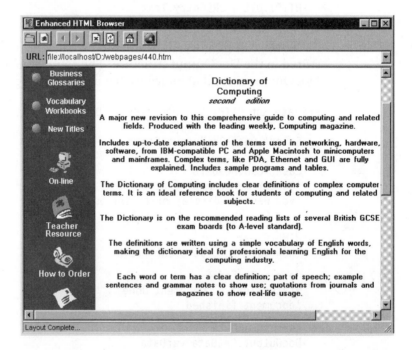

The Command1 button takes the text field of the edit box on the form and passes this to the HTML control that requests the URL entered in this edit box.

Transferring files: The FTP client

The TCP/IP protocol supports file transfers between computers using the file transfer protocol (FTP). If you are running an intranet or if you want to download files over the Internet, you will need an FTP client application that can send text commands to an FTP server. The commands include support for listing the files in a remote directory and transferring a file.

The way you can implement an FTP client application is to use a very similar procedure to that used in the previous examples—again, with the Microsoft ICP components. Once the client has established a socket connection with the remote server—normally using the TCP/IP port 110—then the client and server can exchange information. In theory, this is exactly the same as both SMTP and HTTP connections—and the FTP text commands are not too dissimilar.

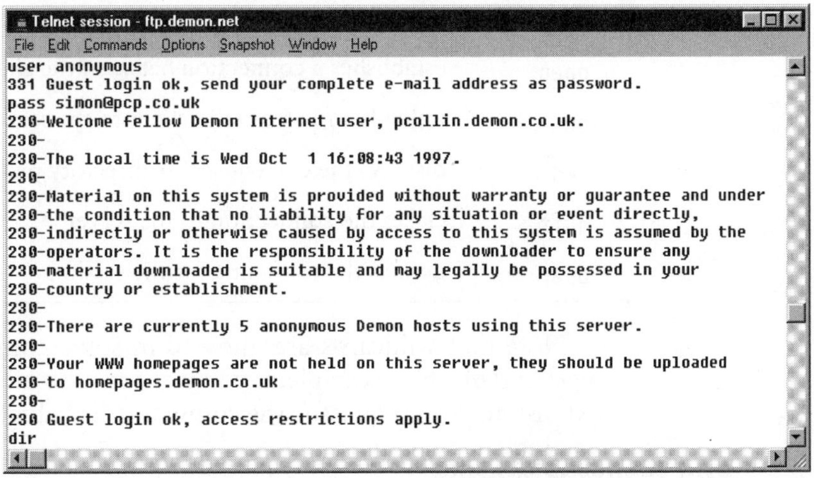

Figure 8.14:
A Telnet
utility
showing
an FTP
conversation.

```
Telnet session - ftp.demon.net                                          _ □ ×
File  Edit  Commands  Options  Snapshot  Window  Help
user anonymous
331 Guest login ok, send your complete e-mail address as password.
pass simon@pcp.co.uk
230-Welcome fellow Demon Internet user, pcollin.demon.co.uk.
230-
230-The local time is Wed Oct  1 16:08:43 1997.
230-
230-Material on this system is provided without warranty or guarantee and under
230-the condition that no liability for any situation or event directly,
230-indirectly or otherwise caused by access to this system is assumed by the
230-operators. It is the responsibility of the downloader to ensure any
230-material downloaded is suitable and may legally be possessed in your
230-country or establishment.
230-
230-There are currently 5 anonymous Demon hosts using this server.
230-
230-Your WWW homepages are not held on this server, they should be uploaded
230-to homepages.demon.co.uk
230-
230 Guest login ok, access restrictions apply.
dir
```

If you are planning on writing an FTP client that accesses a public FTP server, you might run up against an anonymous login. This is really equivalent to a guest login and asks that the user send the user name "anonymous" with their email address as a password.

The FTP.Authenticate method is used to send the user and password details to the server; you could set the anonymous login as an automatic option.

Table 8.1: *The FTP command set*

Command	Meaning
ascii	sets the file transfer mode to ASCII 7-bit transfer
binary	sets the file transfer mode to ASCII 8-bit transfer
cd	change the current directory
close	terminates an FTP session with a server
delete	deletes a named file from the directory
dir	list of the files and directories on the server
get	downloads a file from the server to the client
ls	simple list of the files in a particular directory on the server
mget	downloads multiple files using wildcards
mput	uploads multiple files using wildcards
open	establishes a connection between the client and server
put	uploads a file from the client to the server
pwd	displays the current server directory path
quit	closes the connection to the server
user	defines the username for the session

Note that wildcards are allowed in some commands including ls, mget and dir. For example, if you want to view all files that have a .doc extension, you could issue the command "ls *.doc".

File transfer modes

The default method of transferring files with FTP is ASCII mode. Using this mode is fine for transferring plain text files and for viewing "readme" files, but it can corrupt binary application or multimedia files as the FTP client tries to translate the characters into ASCII text.

FTP reply codes

When an FTP server is asked to carry out a command by an FTP client, it will reply with a three-digit number code that describes whether it can and will carry out the command. It is particularly useful to know the meaning of these reply codes, especially when you are trying to get your FTP server up and running.

Table 8.2: *FTP reply codes*

Number	First Digit	Second Digit
0	n/a	syntax error
1	positive, more information following	information data
2	positive, command completed ready for next command	connection established
3	positive but waiting for rest of command or data	login authentication
4	command not accepted, try again	n/a
5	command not accepted, do not try again	server file system status

The third digit of the reply informs the user about the scale of the status reply defined by the second digit.

Using the FTP control

In our first example, we will create just about the simplest FTP application to log in to a remote FTP server using a guest account.

```
Sub FTP_Login()

    FTP.Connect
    'now, wait until the connection process is complete
    Do While (FTP.State = prcConnecting) or (FTP.State =
        prcResolvingHost) or (FTP.State = prcHostResolved)

        DoEvents
    Loop

    FTP.UserID = "guest"
    FTP.Password = "password"
    FTP.Authenticate

    'wait until the authentication has completed
    Do While FTP.ProtocolState=1)
        DoEvents
    Loop

End Sub
```

You might have noticed similar code from earlier examples, especially as the routine loops waiting for the last task to complete. Just like the SMTP and HTTP clients, this FTP client will manage the incoming data (in this initial case, the listing information) using a routine linked to the new data event ListItem.

Unlike the other client controls, the FTP client can route the incoming data into two different structures—either the ListItem object or a DocOutput object (the same type of object used in mail and Web clients). This choice is controlled by the ListItemNotify property (if set to True, the data will be routed to a ListItem object, if False it is sent to a DocOutput object). The next routine requests a listing of files from the remote server and the third routine manages the data received in the ListItem object.

```
Sub ListFiles()

    'setup to use a ListItem object
    FTP.ListItemNotify = True
    'now list the current remote root directory
    FTP.List FTP.RemoteDir

End Sub
```

Figure 8.15:
A basic FTP client with local and remote files.

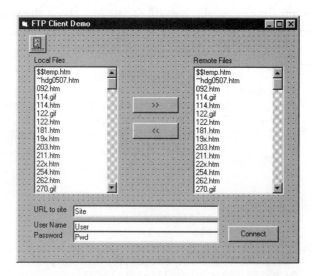

To process the list data that is returned from the routine above, we use an event handler to fill a listbox on our form (called FileList). The routine splits out the directories and files returned from the FTP host by using the Attribute property of the ListItem object entry. If `Attribute=1` the entry is a directory; if `Attribute=2` the entry is a file.

```
Sub FTP_ListItem(ByVal lstData As FTPDirItem)

    if lstData.Attributes = 1 Then
        'entry is a directory
        FileList.AddItem FTP.RemoteDir & "/" & lstData.filename
    Else
        'entry is a file
        FileList.AddItem lstData.filename
    End If

End Sub
```

The `FTPDirItem` provides a number of other elements for each item returned, including the Attribute (used above), Date, Details, Filename, and Size. You can use each of these elements of the object when displaying the results of a listing.

Sending a file is carried out with a single method, PutFile. Similarly, to receive a file use the GetFile method. Lastly, you can change directory on the remote server using the ChangeDir method. An example of two of these methods in use is shown below:

```
Sub Send_File()

    Dim newDirectory As String
    Dim sendFileName As String
    newDirectory = newDirectoryLst.Item
    sendFileName = strFile.Text

    'change directory on the remote server
    FTP.ChangeDir newDirectory

    'wait until the server has finished processing
    Do While FTP.Busy
        DoEvents
    Loop

    'send the file and save with the same name on the remote server
    FTP.PutFile sendFileName sendFileName
    'wait while the file is being transmitted
    Do While FTP.Busy
        DoEvents
    Loop

End Sub
```

This has covered the basics of an FTP client that will work on any TCP/IP network.

Conclusion

In this chapter I have shown you how to use the NetMasters ICP control pack to access the main network functions of a TCP/IP Internet, namely socket connections between client–server applications. I have also shown how to implement some of the common TCP/IP clients, namely to use the HTML control to show how the client–server model would work when requesting a Web page from an HTTP server and how to send a file using the FTP client. I have not covered the remaining TCP/IP servers in this book (notably NNTP for newsgroups) simply because this is a network book rather than an Internet application book! However, with the basic network socket conversation methods described, you should now find it a straightforward matter to develop these applications if you are developing an Internet suite.

9

Advanced Network Communications

Introduction

Creating network applications that can communicate directly over the network is the subject of this chapter. The advanced techniques described here cover ways in which two or more applications can create a channel over the network and exchange information. This is ideal for applications such as groupware and scheduling systems where clients need to check with other clients on the status of an appointment. These functions, generally called interprocess communications, form the basis of any client–server application.

In this chapter, I also cover Network DDE. Much like standard DDE, this system allows one application to launch an application on another client via the network—and has been used in one memorable example to demonstrate distributed computing power of networked PCs to rival a supercomputer! However, for more day-to-day applications it is an excellent and easy-to-use method of sharing information over the network.

Network DDE

Network DDE provides a Dynamic Data Exchange data link over a network. Standard DDE takes place between two different applications on a single machine; for example, calling Microsoft Excel from within Visual Basic. Network DDE enables applications on different machines to communicate; the other main difference is that Network DDE also allows the same application running on different PCs to communicate. This makes the system ideal as a data channel for groupware, scheduling, version control or other systems where each user needs the same application delivered to his desktop. To give you an idea of how Network DDE operates, Windows provides a few simple applications that use Network DDE calls: ClipBook Viewer and ClipBook Server.

Network DDE is implemented using a DLL that ensures that it is independent of the network transport protocol. For example, the Network DDE provided with Windows for Workgroups and Windows 95 includes a NetBIOS interface—if you need a driver for another network protocol, look to the network provider (a good source is the CompuServe vendor support forums). By remaining independent of the protocol layer, the Network DDE calls can route information over the network using a standard set of API calls. It is also designed to look similar to the standard DDE process: if you are already familiar with DDE, then Network DDE will come naturally. To implement Network DDE, you need only make a few changes to the service and topic strings sent in a DDE transaction. Once a conversation is established between the two computers, the DDE transactions are the same as any local transaction—the Network DDE manager intercepts transactions destined for a remote PC and routes them via NetBIOS over the network.

A secondary advantage of Network DDE is that it allows one application to launch an application on another computer—in the same way that DDE can launch an application on the local PC. This means you could produce applications that take advantage of the full power of all the PCs on a network by sharing the processing load; you could also use this system to show an alert, or as an email or diary application.

Naming conventions in Network DDE

Windows and Windows for Workgroups both implement Network DDE by abstracting the connections into a network share. The main function used to create a connection is the DdeConnect() function. The convention is that the application uses a service name in the format "\\machinename\\NDDE$" and a topic name that contains the name assigned to the share, usually with a $ symbol appended to the end of the name, for example "DIARY$". This share name is stored in the SYSTEM.INI file under the [DDEShares] section, which describes the topic provided through that share and the items supported for that topic. Each topic your application supports requires a different share.

Security in Network DDE

One of the benefits of abstracting the connection to a share is that share-level security is available (as it is with other physical resources). Each item in a topic has two passwords that apply to two sets of permission flags. If the connecting peer provides the first password, it's allowed the first set of permissions. If it gives the second password then it's allowed the second set of permissions. This means that you can easily define read-only and read-write permission sets linked to two passwords.

Establishing a Network DDE link

Establishing a Network DDE link involves three basic steps:

1. Add an entry to SYSTEM.INI that identifies the link topic information for the DDE source.
2. Create a DDE source application with a DDE link topic corresponding to the information in the SYSTEM.INI file.
3. Establish a DDE destination link that references the remote computer name and the SYSTEM.INI link topic description.

The first step involves writing a new entry to the SYSTEM.INI file. In the example below, I will use one of the Windows API functions, but you might already have your own routine or library component that does the same job (I happen to prefer the API, since it saves using another library file).

The entry looks rather similar to the following:

```
[DDEShares]
MyDDESource$=MYSource,MySourceAppTopic,,31,,0,,0,0,0
```

where:

MyDDESource$ Name of the network DDE topic that is used as the DDE destination LinkTopic string when the DDE connection is made.

MySource   Name of the DDE source application EXE.

MySourceAppTopic   Name of the DDE source link topic that is the same as the form's LinkTopic property for the source application.

The rest of the numbers are standard permission security default settings.

Figure 9.1:
*Editing the
SYSTEM.INI
file to add a
DDE share
alias.*

```
[System - Notepad
File  Edit  Search  Help
keyboard.drv=keyboard.drv
fonts.fon=vgasys.fon
fixedfon.fon=vgafix.fon
oemfonts.fon=vga850.fon
386Grabber=vgafull.3gr
display.drv=pnpdrvr.drv
mouse.drv=mouse.drv
*DisplayFallback=0
atm.system.drv=system.drv

[DDEShares]
MyDDESource$=MYSource,MySourceAppTopic,,31,,0,,0,0,0

[keyboard]
subtype=
type=4
keyboard.dll=
oemansi.bin=xlat850.bin

[boot.description]
```

The NDDE source application

Our Network DDE source application will be used to send the text you type into an edit box to another application (the destination application) that will display these characters on another PC—not very inspired, but it shows all the principles at work.

Create a new VB program and change the LinkTopic property of the main Form1 form to "MySourceAppTopic". Now change the Link-Mode property of the Form1 to "1 - Source". Add a text box to the form and change its Name property as "TextItem".

To write to the SYSTEM.INI file, I am using the standard Windows API function, WritePrivateProfileString(). To use this method, add the following function definition at the start of the code:

```
Declare Function WritePrivateProfileString Lib "Kernel" (ByVal
lpApplicationName As String, ByVal lpKeyName As String, ByVal
lpString As String, ByVal lplFileName As String) As Integer
```

Now enter the following code for the main Form_Load() routine of the program.

```
Sub Form_Load ()

    Dim retValue As Integer
    Dim szFile As String          ' INI filename.
    Dim szSection As String       ' INI file section title.
    Dim szEntry As String         ' INI file section entry.
    Dim szString As String        ' INI file entry value.
```

```
szFile = "SYSTEM.INI"
szSection = "DDEShares"
szEntry = "MySource$"
szString = "MYSOURCE,MySourceAppTopic,,31,,0,,0,0,0"

' Write this information to the SYSTEM.INI file.
retValue = WritePrivateProfileString(szSection, szEntry,
    szString, szFile)

End Sub
```

Figure 9.2:
Apiary supplies NetBIOS components that provide interprocess communications.

When you make this file into an EXE, be sure to name the file MYSOURCE.EXE.

You can now create the DDE destination application that will display the text you type in the text control of the source in its own text control. Create a new application within VB and add a text box to the main form. The main code looks like:

```
Sub Form_Load ()

    Dim retValue As Long
    Dim szMachine As String      ' Network server name.
    Dim szTopic As String
```

```
'Name of computer on which the source app is running
szMachine = "\\MACHINE1"

'Name of the DDE source item in the SYSTEM.INI on the
'source computer
szTopic = "MySource$"

Text1.LinkMode = 0

' Now define the full link topic string, with the
'application name of NDDE$
Text1.LinkTopic = szMachine + "\" + "NDDE$" + "|" + szTopic
'Now define name of link item in the source application
Text1.LinkItem = "TextItem"
'Now create an automatic NDDE lin
Text1.LinkMode = 1

End Sub
```

Figure 9.3:
A simple
NDDE utility.

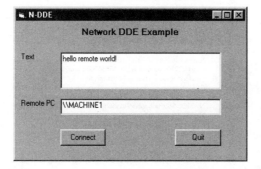

It is important to ensure that the machine name (stored in szMachine) is correct for the PC that is running the source application. You can check this (and set it) using either the Network icon in the Control Panel or by the network APIs described in Chapter 2. If you do not have the correct machine name for the source, you will get an error of "DDE method invoked with no channel."

The App-Link alternative to Network DDE

If you are not too sure that you want to dive into Network DDE, you might consider the third-party component App-Link from Synergy Software, Vermont, USA. App-Link is a VBX/OCX component that provides all the functionality of Network DDE wrapped in a friendly and familiar control. It is programmed using a set of properties that are less forgiving than some of the NDDE settings—for example, you can specify a range of machine names, types of link, and security settings. The control will also work with a range of network protocols other than the usual Microsoft Net-BIOS transport.

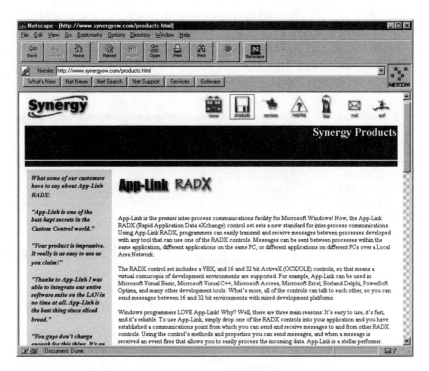

Figure 9.4:
The App-Link component provides a proprietary way of exchanging information between applications.

OLE automation

OLE has become familiar to every programmer and provides a way of linking formatted data from one application to another application. This would seem to be a natural for networking, and it is! All the OLE Automation and Server functions are provided with the Enterprise Edition of Visual Basic, under the name Remote Automation. Since these are a standard feature and are covered in detail in the Microsoft manuals, I am not going to repeat the information in this book. Suffice to say that if you need to use shared OLE objects over a network, you should be using the Enterprise Edition of VB.

Mailslots

Mailslots are an alternative method of providing interprocess communications; like Network DDE and named pipes, they are native to Windows and are accessed from a set of API functions in the Windows SDK library and resource kit. In structure and format, a mailslot looks much like a Network DDE connection and the naming conventions are similar.

By far the simplest way of handling mailslots is to use one of the custom controls available from several third-party developers such as Mabry Software. The Mabry VBX control provides access to all standard mailslot functions, allowing the developer to create a mailslot to another application and then write or read data from the slot.

Figure 9.5:
The Mabry Mailslots component wraps up the Windows API functions.

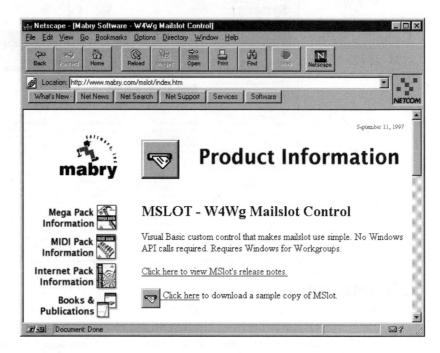

Named pipes

A *named pipe* is a mechanism available in 32-bit Windows platforms that provides a link between two or more applications running on different computers. It is very similar to a mailslot and the functions can be used to access mailslot data. Any VB developers with a background in Windows NT are sure to have come across named pipes, since they are a vital part of the NT communications model.

However, unlike mailslots, there are currently no custom controls that package the named pipe API calls into a developer-friendly component. This means that if you want to use named pipes, you will have to stick to API calls from within the VB application.

Figure 9.6:
*The hard way
of using named
pipes—with
the raw
Windows
API calls.*

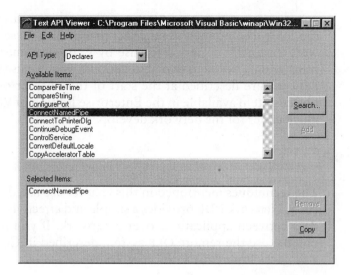

There are several Windows API functions that are used to create and control a named pipe:

```
CallNamedPipe
ConnectNamedPipe
CreateNamedPipe
CreatePipe
DisconnectNamedPipe
GetNamedPipeHandleState
GetNamedPipeInfo
PeekNamedPipe
SetNamedPipeHandleState
TransactNamedPipe
WaitNamedPipe
```

To use any of these functions you should use the techniques described in Chapter 2 to cut and paste the API definition from the Text API Viewer utility into your VB project code.

The simplest way of using a named pipe is as a single communication between a pipe server and a pipe client. The server creates a single pipe using the CreateNamedPipe function, connects to the client, sends the information and then disconnects the pipe and closes the pipe handle. However, it is more usual for the server to communicate with multiple clients, but this requires a slightly different technique. Instead of creating a single pipe to each client in turn, it is far more efficient for the server to create multiple server pipes to each client simultaneously.

For general use, I would suggest that the mailslot control mentioned above provides all the functionality that a VB programmer will need. If you do require a communications channel, a mailslot works fine and the control component is far easier to user than these API functions that were originally designed for use by C programmers. If you need to transfer data between two applications, why not use the easy Network DDE feature described at the start of this chapter or the remote OLE object system available in the Enterprise Edition of VB—both make life much easier for the network developer!

Conclusion

The techniques mentioned in this chapter are listed according to difficulty. Network DDE provides a simple and effective way of exchanging data between applications over a network. If you need to share OLE objects, use the remote OLE system described in Chapter 7 and available in the Enterprise Edition of VB.

For most programmers, mailslots and named pipes will provide useful services but ones that are likely to be rarely used. Although these APIs are documented in the Windows API help system, I would suggest that it is more in keeping with the VB spirit to use one of the control components to wrap up the functions in a friendly set of properties.

Internet Resources

General search engines

Search for the network term then narrow down with VB

Site	*Location*	*Comments*
Excite	www.excite.com	Excellent search engine that provides QBE and links responses to related sites—demonstrates the full version of the search engine available for your own Web server
InfoSeek	www.infoseek.com	One of the most comprehensive directories of Web pages and resources on the Internet
Yahoo!	www.yahoo.com	Provides an excellent listing for most Web sites and FTP stores on the Internet
Lycos	www.lycos.com	An excellent search engine that provides very good coverage of the Internet
Yell	www.yell.co.uk	A search directory with a UK bias, provided by the Yellow Pages
Yahoo! UK	www.yahoo.co.uk	A tailored UK version of the well-known search engine
AltaVista	www.altavista.digital.com	Very good directory with entries for most Web sites and FTP stores—uses a search engine similar to the Private Extensions product available for your own Web server

Newsgroups

Finding newsgroups that relate to Visual Basic

Source	Location	Comments
DejaNews	www.dejanews.com	An excellent directory of all the newsgroups that make up Usenet—lets you search for newsgroups that cover your subject area
TileNet News	www.tilenet.news.com	Another good search directory that lets you find the newsgroup of your choice

Mailing lists

Finding mailing lists that relate to Visual Basic

Source	Location	Comments
Liszt	www.liszt.com	Directory that covers just about every mailing list together with a description and joining details

Standards

Standards and defining companies

Company	Location	Comments
NCSA	hoohoo.ncsa.uiuc.edu	The company that started the WWW process and lists resources and standards for the Web and Internet access
Netscape	www.netscape.com	Developers of the popular Navigator Web browser and Web server software that can be called from VB
Microsoft	www.microsoft.com	Developers of the IE Web browser (plus all the VB range)

Visual Basic sites

Site name	Location	Comments
Carl and Gary's VB Site	www.apexsc.com/vb	Great site that has masses of info and tips on VB programming
Microsoft VB pages	www.microsoft.com/vbasic	You should visit this often for updates, tips and patches
Starting Point for VB	www.vbstart.com	Excellent new service that provides the ideal launch pad for all VB programmers to surf the Web
Visual Basic Programmers Journal	www.windx.com	The VPPJ is a good source of techniques and tips for VB programmers—some sections are subscriber-only

Third-party control developers

Developer	Location	Comments
Apiary	www.apiary.com	Provides Internet, NetWare and NetBIOS libraries
Distinct	www.distinct.com	Develops TCP/IP component libraries
Mabry	www.mabry.com	Provides mailslot control pack together with other communications utilities
NetMasters	www.netmasters.com	This company now handles the ICP suite of controls previously known as the Microsoft ICP
Sheridan	www.sheridan.com	Develops a range of add-in libraries for communications

Index